American Book Company
The Standards Experts

LOUISIANA iLEAP

7TH GRADE

SOCIAL STUDIES

Developed to the Louisiana Performance Standards

Kindred Howard
Katie Herman

American Book Company
PO Box 2638
Woodstock, GA 30188-1383
Toll Free: 1 (888) 264-5877   Phone: (770) 928-2834
Fax: (770) 928-7483   Toll Free Fax: 1 (866) 827-3240
www.americanbookcompany.com

ACKNOWLEDGEMENTS

The authors would like to gratefully acknowledge the formatting and technical contributions of Marsha Torrens and Yvonne Benson.

We also want to thank Charisse Johnson and Eric Field for developing the graphics for this book.

This product/publication includes images from CorelDRAW 9 and 11 which are protected by the copyright laws of the United States, Canada, and elsewhere. Used under license.

Copyright© 2008
by American Book Company
PO Box 2638
Woodstock, GA 30188-1318

ALL RIGHTS RESERVED

The text of this publication, or any part thereof, may not be reproduced or transmitted in any form or by any means, electronic or mechanical, including photocopying, recording, storage in an information retrieval system, or otherwise, without the prior written permission of the publisher.

Printed in the United States of America

05/08

Preface	vii
Diagnostic Test	**1**
Evaluation Chart for Diagnostic Test	15

Chapter 1 United States Geography:
Map Skills and Geographical Impact on History — 17

1.1 The United States in Spatial Terms	17
Maps	17
Types of Maps	17
Reading and Understanding Maps	22
Charts, Graphs, and Diagrams	23
1.2 The Impact of Physical Features and Climate on US History	28
The Atlantic Coast and Appalachian Mountains	28
The Ohio River Valley	29
Prior to US Independence	29
After US Independence	30
The Mississippi River	31
The Great Plains	32
The Rocky Mountains	32
Gold	34
Effects on Native Americans	34
Environmental Concerns	34
Chapter 1 Review	36

Chapter 2 United States Geography: Physical and Human Systems — 39

2.1 Migration, Immigration, and Urban Development	39
Western Migration	39
Urbanization	40
Immigration	41
The Acadians	41
German and Irish Immigrants	42
Chinese Immigrants	42
Late Nineteenth Century Immigration	43
Push and Pull Factors	43
Consequences of Urban Development	43

i

Positive Consequences	43
Negative Consequences	44
Migration, Immigration, and Urbanization Today	45
2.2 Geographical Impact: Economically and Politically	46
Economic Impact	46
Impact of Environment	46
Geography's Impact on Political Boundaries	47
Slavery	47
The Louisiana Purchase	48
The Missouri Compromise	48
Land From Mexico	49
Recap of Geography's Political and Economic Influence	49
Chapter 2 Review	50

Chapter 3 United States Government — 53

3.1 Purpose and Structure of US Government	53
Types of Governments	53
Purposes of US Government	54
Federalism	55
Checks and Balances	56
3.2 Separation of Powers	58
The Legislative Branch – Congress	58
Powers and Limitations of Congress	59
The Executive Branch — The President, Vice President, and Cabinet	61
Responsibilities and Powers of the President and Vice President	62
The President's Cabinet and Joint Chiefs of Staff	62
The Judicial Branch – the Federal Courts	64
3.3 How a Bill Becomes Law	66
Legislative Process	66
Committees and Filibusters	66
Chapter 3 Review	68

Chapter 4 The United States Political System — 71

4.1 Foundations of US Politics	72
Drafting and Ratification of the United States Constitution	72
Articles of Confederation and Shays's Rebellion	72
The Constitutional Convention	73
Ratification	74
Federalists vs. Anti-Federalists	74
The Bill of Rights	75
4.2 Historical Influences on US Government	78
Ancient Models of Government	78
British Influences	79
The Mayflower Compact	79
The Declaration of Independence	80
Principles of Government Embodied in the US Constitution	81
4.3 US Politics in Action	82
Political Parties	82

  Party Structure and Function..82
 Affecting Change in a Democratic Society 83
  Elections 83
  Political Compromise...84
 Citizen Rights and Responsibilities 85
4.4 The United States and Other Nations 87
 Diplomacy and Aid 87
 Trade 88
 Carrying Out US Foreign Policy 89
 Common Foreign Policy Issues 90
 The United Nations 91
Chapter 4 Review 92

Chapter 5 Historical Thinking Skills 95

5.1 Chronological Relationships and Patterns...95
5.2 Impact of People and Events on History 97
 Historical Points of View 97
 Recognizing Causes and Effects in US History..................................98
5.3 Historical Research..100
 Researching Historical Questions 100
 Evaluating Alternatives..101
Chapter 5 Review 102

Chapter 6 US History: Birth of a Nation 103

6.1 The American Revolution 103
 Causes of the Revolution 103
  The Sons of Liberty..104
  Conflict in Boston 105
  The "Shot Heard 'Round the World"..106
 Key Figures of the American Revolution 106
 The First Year of the Revolution 109
  Ticonderoga and Boston...109
  New York and New Jersey...110
 The Northern War..110
  Saratoga and Benedict Arnold..110
  Valley Forge...111
 The Southern War..111
  Yorktown..112
6.2 The Young Country 113
 Early Effects of the Revolution 113
 President George Washington 114
  Hamilton's Economic Plan...114
  Washington and Neutrality...115
 The Rise of Political Parties 116
 John Adams and Thomas Jefferson 117
  The Election of 1800..117
Chapter 6 Review 119

Chapter 7 US History: An Expanding Country — 123

- 7.1 The Nation Moves West 123
  - Opening the Door to Expansion 123
    - The Northwest Territory and Louisiana Purchase 123
    - The War of 1812 124
    - The Monroe Doctrine 126
    - The Oregon Trail 126
    - Relations with Spain 127
  - Manifest Destiny 128
    - Texas: Independence and Annexation 128
    - Oregon 129
    - War with Mexico and the Gadsden Purchase 130
    - California 131
    - Federal Legislation 131
- 7.2 The Impact of Technology and Infrastructure 133
  - Henry Clay's American System 133
  - Cumberland Road and the Erie Canal 134
  - Important Technology 135
    - The Cotton Gin 135
    - The Steel and Mechanical Plow 135
    - The Steamboat 136
    - Railroads 136
- 7.3 Effects of Expansion on Native Americans 138
  - Buffalo and Reservations 138
  - Violent Confrontations 139
    - Sand Creek 139
    - Little Bighorn 139
    - Chief Joseph 140
    - Wounded Knee 140
    - The Dawes Act 141
- Chapter 7 Review 142

Chapter 8 Democracy, Religion, and Reform — 145

- 8.1 Jacksonian Democracy 145
  - A "Corrupt Bargain" 146
  - Universal (White Male) Suffrage 146
- The "Spoils System," Strict Interpretation, and
- Laissez-Faire Economics 146
  - Spoils System 146
  - Laissez-Faire Economics 147
  - Strict Interpretation 147
  - The Kitchen Cabinet 147
  - Indian Removal 148
  - The Battle Over Federal Power 148
    - South Carolina Nullification Crisis 149
  - Return of the Two-Party System 149
- 8.2 Religion and Reform 151
  - The Second Great Awakening 151
  - Reform Movements 151

    Educational Reform.. 151
    Prison and Mental Health Reform... 152
    The Abolitionist Movement 152
    Temperance 153
    Women's Suffrage 153
Chapter 8 Review 155

Chapter 9   US History: Secession, Civil War, and Reconstruction   157

9.1 Regional Differences 157
    Economies of the North and South 157
        Immigrants and "Know-Nothings" 158
    Slavery 159
        The Missouri Compromise.. 159
        The Compromise of 1850.. 159
        The Kansas-Nebraska Act... 160
        The Dred Scott Decision 160
        John Brown's Raid 161
9.2 Secession and Civil War.. 162
    The Republicans and the Election of 1860 162
    Fort Sumter 163
    The Civil War 163
        War Time Advantages... 163
        First Bull Run and the Anaconda Plan 166
        Antietam 166
        The Emancipation Proclamation 167
        Chancellorsville.. 167
        Gettysburg 168
        Vicksburg 168
        Sherman's Atlanta Campaign and March to the Sea............. 169
        Louisiana and the Civil War.. 170
        Union Victory.. 171
9.3 Reconstruction 172
    Presidential Reconstruction 172
    Radical Reconstruction 173
        Johnson's Impeachment 174
    African Americans and Reconstruction....................................... 175
        Sharecropping and Tenant Farming 175
        The Freedmen's Bureau 175
        Education and the Church 176
        Politics, Print, and Social Debate 176
    White Resistance.. 177
        The Klu Klux Klan and the White League........................... 177
        Carpetbaggers and Scalawags 178
    The Compromise of 1877 178
Chapter 9 Review 180

Practice Test 1   183
Practice Test 2   195

PREFACE

Louisiana 7th iLeap Social Studies will help students who are learning or reviewing material for the iLeap exam. The materials in this book are based on the testing standards as published by the Louisiana Department of Education.

This book contains several sections. These sections are as follows: 1) general information about the book; 2) a diagnostic test; 3) an evaluation chart; 4) chapters that teach the concepts and skills that improve graduation readiness; 5) two practice tests. Answers to the tests and exercises are in a separate manual. The answer manual also contains a Chart of Standards for teachers to make a more precise diagnosis of student needs and assignments.

We welcome comments and suggestions about the book. Please contact the authors at

American Book Company
PO Box 2638
Woodstock, GA 30188-1383

Toll Free: 1 (888) 264-5877
Phone: (770) 928-2834
Fax: (770) 928-7483
Web site: www.americanbookcompany.com

Preface

ABOUT THE AUTHORS

Lead Author:

Kindred Howard is a 1991 alumnus of the University of North Carolina at Chapel Hill, where he graduated with a B.S. in criminal justice and national honors in political science. In addition to two years as a probation & parole officer in North Carolina, he has served for over twelve years as a teacher and writer in the fields of religion and social studies. His experience includes teaching students at both the college and high school levels, as well as speaking at numerous seminars and authoring several books on US history, American government, and economics. Mr. Howard is currently completing both a M.A. in history from Georgia State University and a M.A. in biblical studies from Asbury Theological Seminary. In addition to serving as Social Studies Coordinator for American Book Company, Mr. Howard is the president/CEO of KB Howard Writing, Consulting, and Administrative Services and lives in Kennesaw, Georgia, with his wife and three children.

Katie Herman graduated from Kennesaw State University in 2008 with a Bachelor's degree in English. In addition to co-authoring several social studies books for public schools in Georgia and Louisiana, she has worked as a writing tutor and editor for college students. She plans to pursue a Master's degree in Professional Writing, also at Kennesaw State University. Katie currently lives in Woodstock, Georgia.

iLeap 7th Grade Social Studies Diagnostic Test

The purpose of this diagnostic test is to measure your knowledge in social studies. This test is based on the Louisiana iLeap Seventh Grade test in Social Studies and adheres to the sample question format provided by the Louisiana Department of Education.

General Directions:

1. Read all directions carefully.

2. Read each question or sample. Then choose the best answer.

3. Choose only one answer for each question. If you change an answer, be sure to erase your original answer completely.

4. After taking the test, you or your instructor should score it using the evaluation chart following the test. Circle any questions you did not get correct and review those chapters.

Diagnostic Test

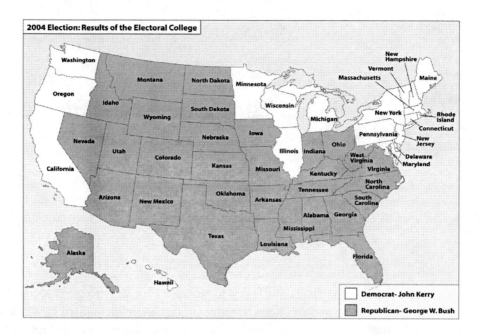

1. Based on the map above, which one of the following statements is definitely true?

   A George W. Bush is a member of the Democratic Party.

   B George W. Bush won the most votes in Ohio.

   C John Kerry ran for Congress in 2004.

   D Most southerners voted for John Kerry.

2. Which of the following examples **best** demonstrates *federalism*?

   A The national government declares war on a foreign country.

   B Congress passes a bill, only to have the president veto it.

   C Congress approves federal money to improve interstate highways, but each state gets to decide what its maximum speed limit will be.

   D The US Supreme Court strikes down a Louisiana law because it rules that the law violates the United States Constitution.

3. In 1787, the delegates to the Constitutional Convention elected to allow slavery in the United States. Which statement **best** describes the effects of this decision?

   A less power for the Federal government

   B divisions between the North and South

   C slavery became prominent in the north

   D industrial economy arose in the south

iLeap 7th Grade Social Studies

Use this passage to answer question 4.

> An act for granting certain taxes in the British colonies and plantations in America; for allowing a drawback of the duties of customs upon the exportation, from this kingdom, of coffee and cocoa nuts the produce of the said colonies or plantations; for discontinuing the drawbacks payable on china earthen ware exported to America; and for more effectually preventing the clandestine running of goods in the colonies and plantations.
>
> – The Townshend Act 1767

4. This passage reflects Britain's purpose in taxing the colonies. Which of the following statements **most accurately** reveals the effects of this act?

   A Most Americans complied peacefully, and it led to better relations between the colonies and Great Britain

   B The Sons of Liberty responded by killing over 100 British soldiers

   C Many American colonists were outraged at these taxes, and it led to the Boston Massacre

   D It led to King George III's Proclamation

5. Under the Missouri Compromise, which of the following was true?

   A Missouri became an independent country until the US could annex it.

   B New northern territories entered the Union as free states, while new southern territories entered as slave states.

   C Citizens of Missouri settled the issue of slavery by popular sovereignty, a decision that reversed the earlier Dred Scott Case.

   D Slaves only counted as three-fifths of a person.

6. The Ohio River Valley is important historically for which of the following reasons?

   A Disagreements over the area helped lead to the American Revolution.

   B It was the site of the nation's largest gold rush in history.

   C Its purchase roughly doubled the size of the country and opened the way for the Lewis and Clark expedition.

   D Conquest of the region completed Manifest Destiny.

7. Which of the following branches of government includes **unelected** officials?

   A executive   C neither A nor B

   B judicial   D both A and B

Diagnostic Test

Use the list of historical events below to answer question 8.

> Thomas Paine publishes *Common Sense* 1776
> Rise of Federalist Party 1792
> George Washington Becomes President 1789
> Boston Massacre 1770
> Start of the American Revolutionary War 1775
> King George III's Proclamation 1763

8 If making a timeline, where would you place the Boston Massacre?

  A Between George Washington Becomes President and the Rise of the Federalist Party.

  B Between King George III's Proclamation and the Start of the American Revolutionary War.

  C Between Thomas Paine publishes *Common Sense* and George Washington Becomes President.

  D Between the Start of the American Revolutionary War and King George III's Proclamation

9 Which of the following statements would a Federalist have **most** agreed with in 1787?

  A "We must be careful not to take power away from the states. A strong national government will lead to oppression."

  B "The government must be limited to only those powers specifically expressed in the Constitution."

  C "Liberty must be protected, indeed. But our young nation requires a strong national government."

  D "Alexander Hamilton's ideas about government are dangerous."

10 Which of the following is the **best** example of checks and balances?

  A Certain powers belong to the states rather than the national government.

  B The president must serve as the head of state and the commander in chief of the military.

  C The House of Representatives may approve a bill, but it cannot go to the president without first passing the Senate as well.

  D Any bill passed by Congress must then go to the president for approval.

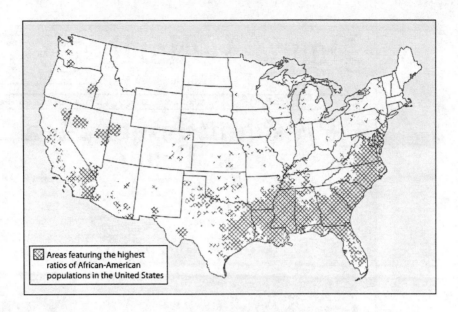

11. Look at the map above. Which of the following offers the **best** explanation of why large numbers of African Americans live where they do?

   A African immigration during the 1800s

   B Historical effects of slavery and urban migration

   C the Monroe Doctrine

   D The consequences of the Dred Scott Case

12. Which of the following was **not** a result of the slavery debate that raged from 1787 until the start of the Civil War?

   A Three-fifths Compromise
   C Dred Scott Case

   B Missouri Compromise
   D Compromise of 1877

13. Which of the following statements **best** describes how white settlers' perception of the Great Plains changed thanks to new farming technology during the 1800s?

   A They stopped viewing the region as a breadbasket and started viewing it as a corn belt.

   B Settlers stopped viewing it as a place to grow cotton and started viewing it as a place to raise cattle.

   C People no longer saw it as a barren desert but as a good land for agriculture.

   D Their image of the region changed very little.

14 The above news article can **best** be described as addressing which of the following?

A US political structure
B the legislative process
C foreign policy issues
D economic aid

15 The invention of the cotton gin is important historically for which of the following reasons?

A forced settlers to relocate to the North
B encouraged Native Americans to attack US settlers
C led to a national identity and the Era of Good Feelings
D fueled support for slavery in new US territories

16 Which of the following would be the **best** heading for a list that includes tenements, slums, dangerous working conditions, and nativism.

A Benefits of Immigration
B Causes of the Civil War
C Negative Consequences of Urban Growth
D Reasons for the Colonies Declared Independence

Process of Appointing Federal Judges

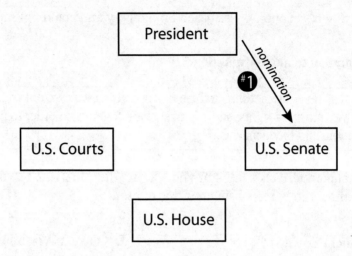

17 The chart above depicts the process by which someone becomes a federal judge. If the nominee is approved, where should arrow number 2 be drawn?

   A from the Senate to the House
   B from the Senate back to the president
   C from the Senate to the courts
   D from the courts to the Senate

18 Which of the following **most likely** contributed to the Indian Removal Policy?   H-1A-M5 H-1B-M9

   A the Emancipation Proclamation
   B Manifest Destiny
   C The Second Great Awakening
   D Spoils System

19 Which of the following **best** explains why the white population of the Oregon Territory grew tremendously following the Lewis and Clark Expedition?   G-1B-M1

   A No human being had ever lived there before.
   B Whites wanted to leave the South after the Emancipation Proclamation.
   C The territory featured available land and gold.
   D Railroads had not yet been invented.

20 Southern exporters opposed US tariffs for which of the following reasons.

   A The South wanted foreign manufactured goods to be priced higher than US goods.

   B The South did not want other countries to respond with tariffs of their own.

   C US tariffs would make cotton more expensive in northern states.

   D The South's economy was based on industry and could not afford tariffs.

Use this quotation to answer question 21

> "The taxes are not fair, and the troops in our cities are not welcome. They are violating our rights, and we must stand together in order to protect our freedom and independence."

21 This quotation reflects a point of view during the American Revolution. Who is **most likely** responsible for this quote?

   A British leader   **C** northern Patriot

   B southern Loyalist   **D** slave in Virginia

22 Which of the following **best** describes the Bill of Rights?

   A ten amendments meant to limit government and protect civil rights

   B natural rights expressed in the Declaration of Independence

   C the very first section of the Constitution to be approved at the Constitutional Convention in 1787

   D laws rejected by the doctrine of nullification

23 Which of the following **best** describes why many colonists reacted with anger towards the Stamp Act?

   A It was a tax that colonists were not allowed to pay.

   B The Stamp Act only allowed colonists to buy stamps at certain times during the year, interfering with colonial business.

   C It was a duty on printed goods that they resented paying.

   D Colonists felt it was a trick by Great Britain to get them to buy British tea.

24 Which of the following events **most directly** helped change the structure of US government?

   A Shays' Rebellion   **C** Civil War

   B Trail of Tears   **D** Louisiana Purchase

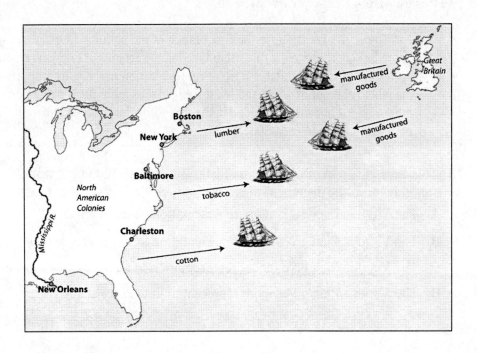

25 What does the picture above illustrate?

   A the economic interdependence between the colonies and Great Britain

   B the effects of the Monroe Doctrine

   C the colonies' financial independence

   D King George's expulsion of the Acadians from Canada

26 Which of the following **most** illustrates separation of powers?

   A Congress makes the law, the president enforces the law, the courts rule on the law.

   B Congress passes a law, but the president vetoes it and sends it back to Congress.

   C Congress has the power to make money and establish post offices.

   D Certain powers belong to the states, certain powers belong to the federal government, and some are shared by both.

27 Which of the following was **least** influenced by the American Revolution?

   A Hamilton's Economic Plan

   B Whiskey Rebellion

   C Trail of Tears

   D proclamation of neutrality

Use this quotation to answer question 10.

> "The right of suffrage in the first branch of the national Legislature ought not to be according to the rule established in the articles of confederation: but according to some equitable ratio of representation namely, in proportion to the whole number of white and other free citizens including three fifths of all other persons not comprehended in the foregoing description, except Indians, not paying taxes in each State."

28 This excerpt is part of the Virginia Plan. With which statement would a person in favor of the document **most likely** agree?

   A The Virginia Plan gives more representation to smaller states.

   B The Virginia Plan gives more representation to larger states.

   C The Virginia Plan gives equal representation to all states.

   D The Virginia Plan gives more representation to slave states.

29 The picture above **most likely** depicts which of the following?

   A western cowtowns

   B the urban north of 1850

   C the southern economy of 1850

   D Radical Reconstruction

30. Jerry and Allison meet with other delegates from their political party in New Orleans, Louisiana. It is the first time in four years that delegates from all over the nation have gathered for such a meeting. At their meeting, they nominate a candidate for president and decide on a set of policies their party will support. Among these are equal rights for foreign immigrants, restrictions on gun ownership, and limits on trade. Which of the following statements is **true**?

   A the meeting is a party platform; the set of policies is the party plank; and trade limits are an issue.

   B the meeting is the party platform; Jerry is a presidential candidate; and Allison supports immigration rights.

   C the meeting is the party convention; the set of policies is the party platform; and restrictions on gun control is a plank.

   D Jerry and Allison are both nominees for president; the party probably opposes tariffs; and the party favors nativism.

31. Abolitionists such as John Brown believed that

   A slavery was immoral and must be stopped immediately.

   B slavery should be ended in gradual steps to prevent chaos.

   C slavery should only be allowed in Georgia and Alabama.

   D only Native Americans should be used as slaves.

> "We the people of the United States, in order to form a more perfect union, establish justice, insure domestic tranquility, provide for the common defense, promote the general welfare, and secure the blessings of liberty to ourselves and our posterity, do ordain and establish this Constitution for the United States of America."
>
> – Preamble to the United States Constitution 1787

32. According to the Preamble to the Constitution, which of the following is a valid role of government?

   A protecting leaders from the people

   B maintaining a military for defense

   C imprisoning those who speak out against the state

   D making sure people make a certain amount of money each year

33. Which of the following is the **best** way citizens can bring about change in a democratic society?

   A rebel against the king

   B secede from the union

   C participate in elections

   D nullify laws

34 The president of the United States is concerned that trade relations with China are not good for US manufacturers. He sits down and peacefully discusses the problem with Chinese leaders in order to come to a solution both countries can accept. What is this process called?

    A. sanction   B. embargo   C. humanitarian aid   D. diplomacy

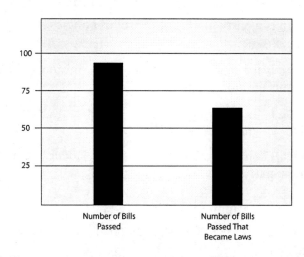

35 The graph above depicts the number of bills passed by Congress in a given year and the number of bills passed that became law. Which of the following **best** explains the difference in height between the two bars on the graph?

    A The Senate was not in session.

    B It was an election year.

    C The president vetoed almost thirty bills.

    D Congress did not send all the bills to the president.

36 Which of the following is **most** responsible for US foreign policy?

    A. Congress

    B. the president

    C. ambassadors

    D. the US military

37 Which of the following is **least likely** to qualify as a US citizen?

    A a twenty-one-year-old immigrant who has been naturalized

    B a Spanish-speaking child born in Peru whose mother grew up in Mississippi

    C a Canadian teenager who has been in the US for less than a year

    D a baby born to Mexican parents in southern Arizona

38 The cartoon above is **most likely** addressing which of the following issues?

   A freedom of religion

   B right to assemble

   C rights of the disabled

   D humanitarian aid

39 What contributed **most** to the Civil War?

   A issues over slavery

   B the industrial economy of the South

   C the Great Depression

   D issues over land ownership

40 What was the significance of the Fourteenth Amendment?

   A It ended slavery throughout the United States.

   B it made African Americans citizens.

   C It guarantees that no citizen may be denied the right to vote.

   D It pardoned the southern states that had seceded from the Union.

41 Which of the following statements describes sectional differences during the War of 1812?

   A New Englanders united with southerners to fight the British.

   B Many US citizens wanted war with the British, but Native Americans considered the British an ally.

   C Southern and western farmers tended to support the war, whereas New England businessmen tended to oppose it.

   D The North was an industrial society that depended heavily on Irish immigrants, while the South depended on slavery.

42 Why were the Cumberland Road and Erie Canal important?

   A Both opened new territory and markets, allowing western settlement to continue at a faster rate.

   B The Union used both to surround the Confederates at Appomatox and end the Civil War.

   C Both opened new paths through the Rocky Mountains

   D Lewis and Clark followed both on their trek through the North American west.

43 Which of the following contributed to **both** western expansion and sectional differences between the North and South?

   A Manifest Destiny

   B the cotton gin

   C the Oregon Trail

   D Presidential Reconstruction

EVALUATION CHART FOR GEORGIA 7TH GRADE ILEAP SOCIAL STUDIES DIAGNOSTIC TEST

Directions: On the following chart, circle the question numbers that you answered incorrectly, and evaluate the results. These questions are based on the *standards and benchmarks published by the Louisiana Department of Education*. Then turn to the appropriate chapters, read the explanations, and complete the exercises. Review other chapters as needed. Finally, complete the Practice test(s) to assess your progress and further prepare you for the **iLeap 7th Grade Social Studies test**.

Note: Some question numbers may appear under multiple chapters because those questions require demonstration of multiple skills.

Chapter		Diagnostic Test Question(s)
Chapter	1: US Geography: Map Skills and Geographical Impact on History	1, 6, 13, 19, 29
Chapter	2: US Geography: Physical and Human Systems	4, 16, 20, 25
Chapter	3: United States Government	2, 7, 10, 17, 23, 32, 35
Chapter	4: The United States Political System	9, 11, 12, 14, 22, 24, 26, 30, 33, 34, 36, 37, 38
Chapter	5: Historical Thinking Skills	3, 18, 21, 28, 39
Chapter	6: US History: Birth of a Nation	8, 21, 22, 27
Chapter	7: US History: An Expanding Country	18, 41, 42, 43
Chapter	8: Democracy, Religion, and Reform	15, 31
Chapter	9: US History: Seccession, Civil War, and Reconstruction	5, 12, 40

Diagnostic Test

# Chapter 1
United States Geography: Map Skills and Geographical Impact on History

This chapter addresses the following Louisiana iLeap standards:

G-1A-M2:	1. Analyze various types of maps, charts, graphs, and diagrams related to U.S. history.
G-1B-M1:	2. Explain how physical features and climate affected migration, settlement patterns, and land use in the United States through 1877.
G-1B-M2:	3. Identify and describe significant physical features that have influenced U.S. historical events (e.g., Ohio River Valley in the American Revolution).
G-1B-M4:	4. Explain ways in which goals, cultures, interests, inventions, and technological advances have affected perceptions and uses of places or regions in the United States.

1.1 THE UNITED STATES IN SPATIAL TERMS

MAPS

Geography is the study of land, bodies of water, people, cultures, climates, and physical features like mountains and plains. When we study **US geography**, we are studying these things as they relate to the United States of America. In order to understand geography, it is important to know how to read and interpret maps. A **map** is an image of a part of the earth. A map of the United States is an image of the US. A US map is very helpful when trying to understand the geography of the United States.

Studying Geography

TYPES OF MAPS

Different types of maps are used to help us understand US geography. A **territorial map** outlines the United States by different territorial regions. The following maps are examples of territorial maps:

- Map #1 outlines the US by states.
- Map #2 outlines the US by commonly recognized geographic regions.
- Map #3 outlines the US by economic regions.

17

United States Geography: Map Skills and Geographical Impact on History

Map #1 :

The US States Outlined

Map #2:

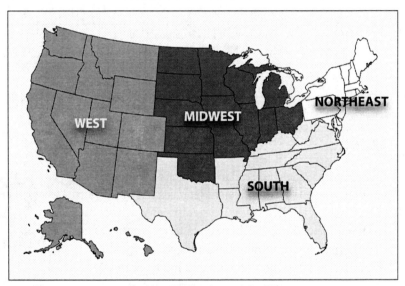

Geographic Regions of the US

Map #3:

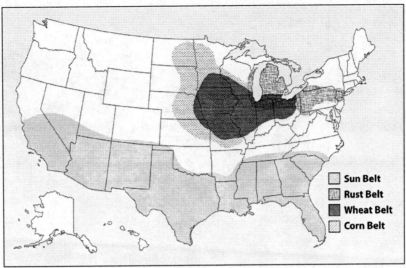

Economic Regions of the US

Sun Belt	Currently, the fastest growing part of the country economically and in terms of population.
Rust Belt	US region that has traditionally relied on industries like steel and automobile production.
Wheat Belt and Corn Belt	Areas of the nation that have traditionally relied on agriculture.

A **population map** depicts where people live. It may reflect US population as a whole, or depict only portions of the country's population. Maps #4 and #5 are examples of population maps:

- Map #4 shows which areas are the most heavily populated in the United States.
- Map #5 shows which states experienced the largest growth in Hispanic population between the years 1990 and 2000.

Map #4:

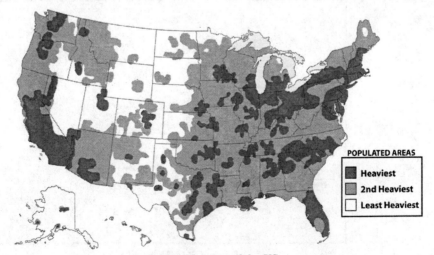

Populated Areas of the US

Map #5:

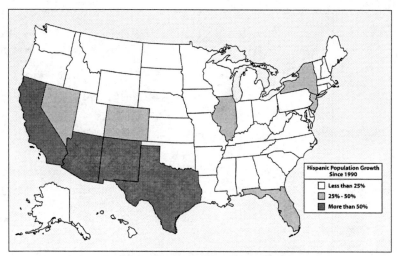

US Hispanic Population 1990–2000

A **topographical map** shows land features like mountains, plains, rivers, and so on.

Mississippi Mountains

Great Salt Lake

- Map #6 is an example of a topographical map of the United States.

Map #6

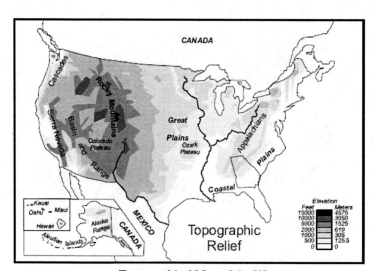

Topographical Map of the US

Chapter 1

People who are interested in politics often study **electoral maps**. Electoral maps outline an area by political factors. For instance, an electoral map may show where different voting districts lie, what portions of the country tend to vote for the Democratic versus the Republican Party during elections, or how many electoral votes states have during presidential elections. Maps #7 and #8 are both examples of electoral maps.

President Bush Being Inaugrated

- Map #7 shows how many electoral votes each state had during the presidential election of 2004.
- Map #8 shows which states voted Republican and which ones voted Democrat during the presidential election of 2004.

Map #7:

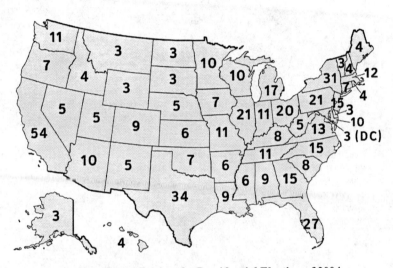

Electoral Votes During the Presidential Election of 2004

Map #8:

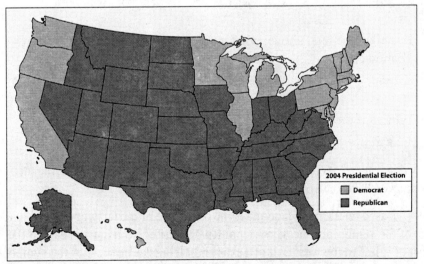

States Voting Democrat and Republican During the Presidential Election of 2004

21

United States Geography: Map Skills and Geographical Impact on History

READING AND UNDERSTANDING MAPS

In order to accurately read a map, you must know what type of map you are looking at and understand its **map key**. Sometimes called a *legend*, the map key is an area, usually right below the map, which tells you what the map's symbols mean. It tells you what images on the map represent mountains, plains, forests, railroads, borders, cities, state capitals, and so on. Look at the map of the United States below. Using the map key, see if you can answer the three questions that follow.

Map Key of the US

1. Based on the map above, which state lies entirely east of the Mississippi River?
    A. Nebraska   B. Texas   C. Georgia   D. Louisiana

2. Based on the map above, what would one find in western North Carolina and eastern Tennessee?
    A. plains   B. major rivers   C. prairies   D. mountains

3. Which of these states would likely offer the best skiing?
    A. Kansas   B. South Dakota   C. Iowa   D. Colorado

How did you do? Were you able to understand the map key, look at the map, and come up with the answers? The correct answers are as follows:

1. – **C**: Based on the map, Georgia is the only state of the answer choices that is located entirely east of the symbol for the Mississippi River. Part of Louisiana is east of the Mississippi, but most of it lies to the west. All of Texas and Nebraska lie west of the symbol representing the Mississippi River on the map.

2. – **D**: Western North Carolina and eastern Tennessee are both covered by the symbol for the Appalachian Mountains. There is no symbol showing major rivers, plains, or prairies located in these states.

3. – **D**: The symbols on the map show that part of the Rocky Mountains runs through Colorado. There are no symbols suggesting mountain ranges in South Dakota, Kansas, or Iowa. Since we know that mountains are necessary for good skiing, the answer must be Colorado.

CHARTS, GRAPHS, AND DIAGRAMS

Charts, graphs, and diagrams are basically pictures of information. They use shapes, colors, lines, and columns to organize and display information in a way that hopefully makes it easier to understand. A **bar graph** uses bars to communicate information. Its bars may be either horizontal (sideways) or vertical (up and down). The following are examples of both a vertical and a horizontal bar graph. The horizontal graph compares US population counts for every fifty years since 1800. The vertical graph compares the average incomes of US citizens based on education levels. See if you can understand the graphs and complete the following statements.

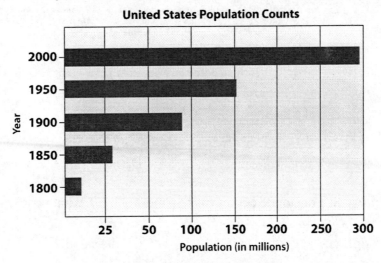

US Population From 1800–2000

1. In 1900, the US population was between _____ and _____ million.
   A. 50 and 100   B. 25 and 50   C. 100 and 200   D. 10 and 30

2. The US population was roughly 80 million in _____.
   A. 1800   B. 1850   C. 1900   D. 1950

3. Between 1950 and 2000 the US population _____.
   A. declined
   B. tripled
   C. remained stable
   D. roughly doubled

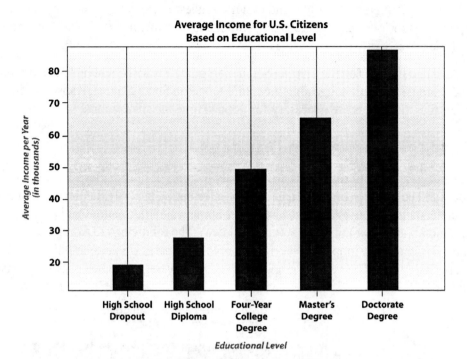

Income Based on Education Level in the US

4. People who make the most money tend to have _____.

   A. less than four years of college
   B. only a high school diploma
   C. a masters or doctorate degree
   D. no formal education

5. People with a doctorate degree make almost _____ what people with a four-year degree make.

   A. four times   B. twice   C. the same   D. three times

6. Someone who graduates with four years of college will, on average, make roughly _____ more dollars a year than a US citizen who only graduates from high school.

   A. $5,000   B. $30,000   C. $100,000   D. $20,000

The answers are as follows:

1. – **A**: Since the bar next to *1900* extends to somewhere between the vertical lines labeled *50* and *100* on the graph, we know that the answer is between 50 and 100 million people.

2. – **C**: Since the bar next to *1900* is the only one that stops just short of the vertical line labeled *100*, it is closer to where *80* would be than any other bar on the graph. Therefore, we know that the answer is *1900*.

Chapter 1

3. – **D**: The bar next to *1950* extends to the vertical line labeled *150*. The bar next to *2000* extends almost as far as the vertical line labeled *300*. 300 – 150 = 150. Therefore, since the difference between the two years is equal to the population in 1950, we know that the answer is *roughly doubled*.

4. – **C**: Looking at the graph, we notice that the higher the bars go, the more money people make. Therefore, since the highest bars are above the categories labeled *masters degree* and *doctorate degree*, we know that the answer is *a masters or doctorate degree*.

5. – **B**: The bar above *doctorate degree* extends well above *$80,000*, but not nearly high enough to be above *$100,000*. Meanwhile, the four-year degree bar only goes as high as around *$50,000*. Therefore, since people with a doctorate clearly make more, but definitely not more than twice as much, we know that the answer is *twice*.

6. – **D**: The bar above *four-year degree* rises to about the per*$50,000 per year* mark. The bar above *high school diploma* rises to just below the *$30,000 per year* mark. Since 50,000 – 30,000 = 20,000, we know that the answer is *$20,000*.

Circle and line graphs are also commonly used to communicate information. Following is an example of each.

- The circle graph shows US population in terms of people's first language.
- The line graph shows average US consumer price index (amount of money people pay for the things they buy) for a given year.

Hispanic Citizens in the US

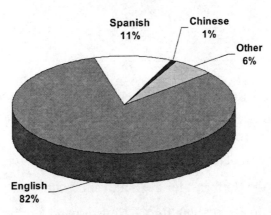

Population Based on First Language

United States Geography: Map Skills and Geographical Impact on History

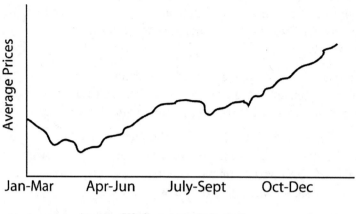

Average US Consumer Price Index

Practice 1.1: The United States in Spatial Terms

Look at the map below and answer questions #1 and #2

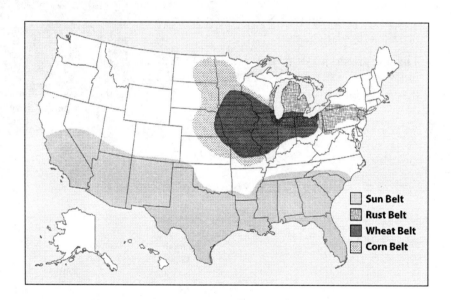

1. Recent statistics show that over the last twenty years, the Sun Belt has been the fastest growing region in the United States. Based on this information, it would appear that people are

    A. moving east of the Mississippi River.

    B. leaving the Northeast for the South and Southwest.

    C. leaving the Deep South for the Midwest and Northeast.

    D. speaking Spanish more than they used to.

2. The northeast United States has traditionally been home to
   A. factories and industry.
   B. large farms that make the region dependent on agriculture.
   C. beaches and warm weather.
   D. the Great Plains.

Look at the circle graph and answer question #3

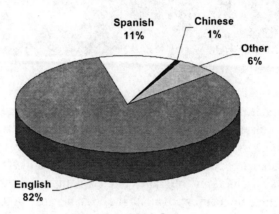

* Based on 2000 Census

3. The circle graph offers evidence that
   A. more US citizens speak Spanish today than last year.
   B. most US citizens speak more than one language.
   C. the US is greatly impacted by its English heritage.
   D. only 1% of US citizens are of Chinese heritage.

1.2 THE IMPACT OF PHYSICAL FEATURES AND CLIMATE ON US HISTORY

THE ATLANTIC COAST AND APPALACHIAN MOUNTAINS

Colonial Jamestown

Colonial New York

Geography has played a key role in US history. Physical features, such as mountain ranges, rivers, water supplies, and so forth, have greatly impacted where people migrated and settled throughout the centuries. Initially, most European colonists settled along the Atlantic coast. The coast was accessible from the sea. Settlers did not have to travel very far inland once they arrived. As a result, early colonists established settlements like Jamestown, Virginia and Plymouth, Massachusetts along the shores of the Atlantic. Eventually, major cities like Boston, New York, and Philadelphia grew up along the coast because of the access to foreign trade their locations offered.

Daniel Boone

As more settlers arrived and land became scarce, European colonists began moving west. At first natural barriers like forests and the **Appalachian Mountains** presented challenges that kept most settlers living in eastern North America. The Appalachian Mountains run from northern Georgia all the way to Maine. During colonial times, the thick forests and high elevations of the Appalachians proved too difficult for most settlers to overcome. Beyond the Appalachians, the land was mostly occupied by Native Americans. Many white settlers and businessmen, however, wanted the land, natural resources, and freedom that awaited them beyond the Appalachians. In 1775, a company hired **Daniel Boone** to forge a route through the Appalachian Mountains to what eventually became Kentucky. Boone's efforts opened up a new path to the west and led to the settlement of vast new territories. People migrated to areas where land was abundant and fertile. Most early settlements and eventual cities grew up along the shores of rivers that allowed people to remain in contact with the more populated areas of the east. These water routes helped settlers engage in trade and travel between the western frontier and eastern towns.

Chapter 1

THE OHIO RIVER VALLEY

PRIOR TO US INDEPENDENCE

Ohio River Valley

The Ohio River and its surrounding territories make up the **Ohio River Valley**. Few regions have played a more important role in US history. Long before any Europeans arrived, Native American peoples inhabited the area for generations. Following colonization, both French and British settlers desired the territory because of the rich land and resources it offered. Tensions between the two nations grew after King George II of Great Britain authorized more British settlement in 1749. Hoping to gain an upper hand, both sides worked to form alliances with Native Americans in the region. Eventually, France and Great Britain went to war. The **French and Indian War** raged from 1754 until 1763. It was part of a world-wide conflict fought between Great Britain and France. Eventually, the British won and gained control of the Ohio River Valley.

After the war, the territory continued to be a source of tension, however. Following the defeat of France and its Native American allies, British colonists wanted to move north of the Ohio River and occupy previously French areas. King George III issued the **Proclamation of 1763.** He outlawed settlement and placed the region under the control of his army. The king wanted time to improve relations with Native Americans who did not trust white settlers. British colonists, however, resented the king, and many ignored his proclamation.

King George III

The Boston Tea Party

By the 1770s, other disputes contributed to protests against the king. When a group of colonists in Boston raided British ships and dumped tea into Boston Harbor, Britain's parliament responded with a series of acts meant to punish the colonies. One of these acts made portions of the Ohio River part of Canada (also a British colony). The colonists were furious! Calls for independence increased. Disputes over the Ohio River Valley eventually helped lead to the **American Revolution**.

AFTER US INDEPENDENCE

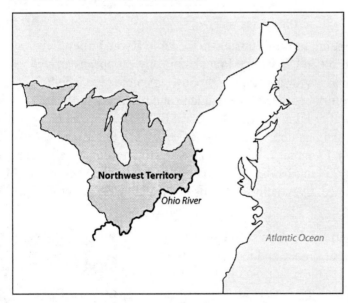

The Northwest Territory

Following the American Revolution, Congress passed the **Northwest Ordinance** in 1787. The law divided the land north of the Ohio River (known as the Northwest Territory) into smaller areas and provided guidelines by which they could one day become states. Ohio, Indiana, Illinois, Michigan, and Wisconsin all formed from these territories.

In the 1700s, many white landowners had slaves. **Slavery** was a system in which blacks in the US were owned like property. The Northwest Ordinance made slavery illegal north of the Ohio River (slave owners living in the territory prior to the law, however, did not have to give up their slaves). While this encouraged many free blacks to move into the territory, it also concerned white settlers who did not want to compete with African Americans for land and work. As a result, white authorities passed a number of laws making it difficult for blacks to move in, such as making them pay money if they did not own land.

As settlers continued moving west, the Ohio River became an important water route. Countless settlers used the river to travel west. Meanwhile, traders, farmers, and merchants relied on it to transport their goods. The Ohio was so traveled that it became a haven for pirates. Pirates raided boats, often killing their victims before taking whatever wealth they could find onboard.

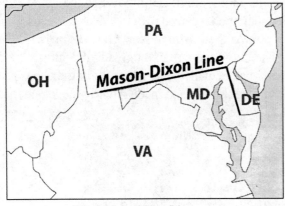
The Mason-Dixon Line

The Underground Railroad

As part of the Mason-Dixon Line, the Ohio River also played a major part in the American **Civil War**. The Mason-Dixon Line served as the boundary between the slaveholding South and the North, where slavery was illegal. The Ohio River Valley became a hotbed of conflict as blacks fled slavery in the southern portions of the Ohio River Valley for freedom across the river. Both before and during the Civil War, the Ohio River Valley played a major role in the Underground Railroad. The **Underground Railroad** was not really a railroad, but rather a series of secret stops along a pathway taken by escaped slaves as they headed north. More slaves fled the South through the Ohio River Valley than through any other area of the country.

THE MISSISSIPPI RIVER

The Mississippi River and Louisiana Territory

Perhaps no river has been more important in US history than the **Mississippi River**. The Mississippi runs south from Minnesota to the Gulf of Mexico. Traditionally, people view the Mississippi as a natural dividing line between the eastern and western United States. For centuries, the river has played an important role in travel and trade because it allows ships to sail back and forth between the Gulf of Mexico and the interior of central North America. President Thomas Jefferson recognized the importance of controlling access to the Mississippi River. He bought New Orleans, the port city at the mouth of the Mississippi, and a vast amount of territory west of the Mississippi River from France in 1803. The deal became known as the **Louisiana Purchase** and made New Orleans an important US city. When the United States went to war with Great Britain in 1812, it understood the need to defend New Orleans. Whoever controlled the city controlled the Mississippi. At the **Battle of New Orleans** in 1815, General Andrew Jackson won a key US victory. The US forces suffered only eight deaths while the British suffered over 700. Although a treaty had actually been signed ending the war prior to the battle, the victory gave people in the US great pride and made Andrew Jackson a national hero.

General Andrew Jackson at the Battle of New Orleans

THE GREAT PLAINS

Eventually, white settlers discovered the **Great Plains** of the Midwest. At first, they thought the Great Plains were nothing more than a worthless desert region. The land was flat, few trees existed, and the ground was too hard to farm. However, with innovative farming techniques and new technology, the Great Plains soon proved to be an abundant region for agriculture and cattle ranching.

THE ROCKY MOUNTAINS

Map of the Rocky Mountains

Full of green forests, a variety of wildlife, and beautiful scenery, the **Rocky Mountains** stretch from New Mexico all the way into Canada. The Rockies were inhabited by Native Americans for thousands of years before white explorers arrived. In 1540, Francisco de Coronado of Spain became the first European known to have explored the region. Almost 200 years later, French explorers ventured west from the Great Plains and discovered the Rockies. By the end of the century, "mountain men" (pioneers who roamed the Rocky Mountains) lived scattered throughout the territory, moving from place to place, trapping animals for their fur, and searching for gold. In 1793, Sir Alexander Mackenzie became the first European to successfully cross the Rockies in modern-day Canada. Before Mackenzie, the Rockies served as a barrier between eastern settlers and the Pacific Ocean. With Mackenzie's success, Europeans and US citizens realized that it was possible to move beyond the Rocky Mountains in their quests for new lands.

The Rocky Mountains

Lewis and Clark

The **Lewis and Clark Expedition** played a major role in opening up the Rockies and the regions beyond to western settlement. President Thomas Jefferson commissioned Meriwether Lewis to find a water route to the Pacific Ocean. Lewis chose William Clark to help him. Their expedition set out from St. Louis, Missouri, in 1804. It followed the Missouri, Yellowstone, and Columbus Rivers west, crossing the Rocky Mountains in modern-day Montana and Idaho. Lewis and Clark conducted the first scientific study of the mountains. They collected plant specimens, studied wildlife, and gathered samples of rocks and soil. The publicity they received and their tales of adventure made US citizens aware of the abundant land and resources in the **Oregon Territory** (region of North America that covered what is today the northwest United States). Lewis and Clark's route west became known as the **Oregon Trail**. Beginning in the mid-1800s, thousands of settlers followed it as they migrated west.

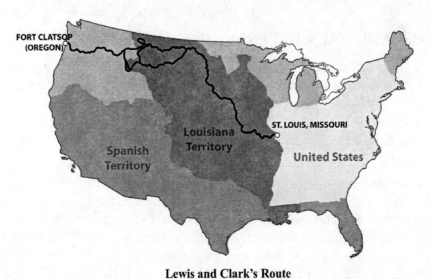

Lewis and Clark's Route

Gold

The Gold Rush

In 1848, settlers discovered **gold** in California. The following year, a massive *gold rush* occurred. A gold rush is when large numbers of people rush to an area where gold has recently been discovered in hopes of striking it rich. Gold rushes cause previously low populated areas to boom in population quickly. The **California Gold Rush** produced just such a boom. These new arrivals came to be known as "49ers" because they arrived in 1849. Ten years later, miners discovered gold in the Rocky Mountains as well. The Rockies produced even more gold than California, and mining soon became the region's first major industry. Small mining settlements cropped up throughout the range. Many of them grew into bustling cities. The completion of the **Transcontinental Railroad** (first cross-country railroad in the United States) in 1869 only added to the Rockies' population explosion. In just over a decade, the Rocky Mountains went from a wilderness occupied by Native Americans, mountain men, and a few pioneer families to a territory featuring growing towns and industries.

Effects on Native Americans

Sadly, white citizens' desire for land and discoveries of gold had tragic consequences for Native Americans. The US government forced many Native Americans out of areas they had occupied for centuries. Without modern weapons and with no political rights (Native Americans were not US citizens and couldn't vote), Native Americans found themselves forced to move to assigned areas (reservations) every time whites wanted more land or found gold. Many Native Americans suffered and died as a result. (We will discuss the effects of western expansion on Native Americans more in Chapter 6).

Environmental Concerns

White settlers moved west for many reasons. Some desired land. Others sought religious freedom. Still others dreamed of finding an abundance of gold. Settlers migrated to places they thought offered these opportunities. They tended to settle in places that offered vegetation, fertile land, and adequate rainfall. At times they had to battle harsh conditions, such as blizzards in the Rockies, or dry, hot deserts in places like New Mexico, Nevada, and parts of Arizona and California.

As the western population increased, so did concerns about the welfare of the environment. Some **conservationists** (people who want to protect the natural environment and limit the use of natural resources) feared massive **deforestation**. Deforestation is the clearing of forest land to make way for human settlement and economic development. As mining and lumber became major industries in the West, many conservationists believed too much forest land was being destroyed. In 1872, the federal government established **Yellowstone National Park** as the nation's first government-protected national park. Twenty years later, President Benjamin Harrison approved the establishment of several Rocky Mountain forest reserves. A decade after that, President Theodore Roosevelt, one of the most passionate conservationists to ever occupy the White House, signed additional legislation protecting western forest areas. Today, environmental issues surrounding the use of western forest lands and natural resources still cause political and scientific debate. Many environmentalists (people devoted to protecting the environment) voice concerns about deforestation and the impact of modern industries. Environmental issues will likely remain an important topic in US society for years to come.

Logging in the 1800s

President Benjamin Harrison

President Theodore Roosevelt

Practice 1.2: The Impact of Physical Features and Climate on US History

1. Why did white settlers initially want to move beyond the Appalachian Mountains?

    A. They believed the best land could be found east of the Appalachians.

    B. They wanted access to the Atlantic coast.

    C. They wanted land and resources.

    D. They wanted to live in one of the new states.

2. The Ohio River Valley played a key role in the American Revolution because
   A. the king's resistance to letting people settle in the region caused anger against Great Britain.
   B. the final battle of the war took place in the region.
   C. George Washington was from the territory.
   D. colonists were angered that the king would make them pick up and move to the territory after the French and Indian War.

3. What was so important about the Ohio River before and during the Civil War?

4. What was the Lewis and Clark Expedition and what impact did it have?

CHAPTER 1 REVIEW

Key Terms, People, and Concepts

geography
US geography
map
territorial map
population map
topographical map
electoral map
map key
charts, graphs, and diagrams
bar graph
circle and line graphs
Appalachian Mountains
Daniel Boone
Ohio River Valley
French and Indian War
Proclamation of 1763
Ohio River Valley's role in American Revolution
Northwest Ordinance

slavery
Ohio River Valley's role in Civil War
Underground Railroad
Mississippi River
Louisiana Purchase
Battle of New Orleans
Great Plains
Rocky Mountains
Lewis and Clark Expedition
Oregon Territory
Oregon Trail
gold
California Gold Rush
Transcontinental Railroad
effects on Native Americans
conservationists
deforestation

Yellowstone National Park

Chapter 1

Multiple Choice Questions

Look at the map below and answer the following question.

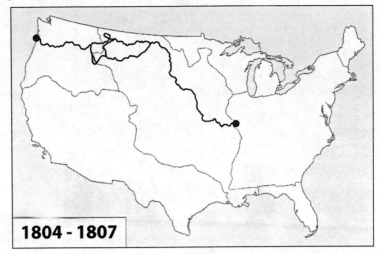

1. The map most likely shows

    A. electoral votes from the presidential election won by Thomas Jefferson.

    B. Daniel Boone's route through the Appalachians.

    C. the Lewis and Clark Expedition.

    D. the path of the Underground Railroad.

2. Which of the following would most upset someone concerned about deforestation?

    A. Native Americans forced to move because whites want land.

    B. a pathway being cleared through the Rockies to build a road.

    C. a lumber company closing.

    D. pirates raiding boats on the Ohio River.

3. Prior to Lewis and Clark, many US citizens viewed the Rockies as

    A. a natural barrier too difficult to cross.

    B. an imaginary place that did not really exist.

    C. a desert region with no use.

    D. part of the French Empire.

Look at the graph below and answer the following question.

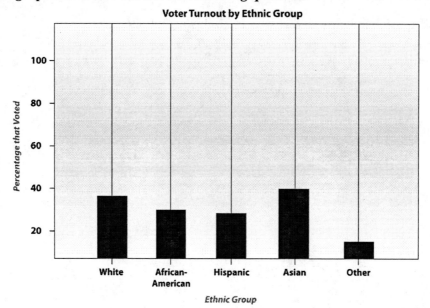

4. What type of graph is this?

   A. line   B. bar   C. circle   D. diagram

5. Based on the same graph as #4, which of the following statements is true?

   A. Less than 20% of the Hispanic population voted.

   B. Roughly half of the white population voted.

   C. Asians had the highest percentage of voter turnout.

   D. The number of whites and African Americans who voted were roughly the same.

6. The Mississippi River has historically been important because it

   A. divides the US between North and South.

   B. formed part of the Mason-Dixon Line.

   C. was a major part of Lewis and Clarks journey west.

   D. allows goods to be transported from the Gulf of Mexico to the interior of the United States.

7. Historically, which of the following areas has been LEAST attractive to US settlers?

   A. coastlines   C. deserts
   B. areas rich in gold D. fertile farmland

8. If one wanted to look at voting patterns over the last three presidential elections, it might be useful to study

   A. economic diagrams. C. electoral maps.
   B. proclamations.   D. migration patterns.

Chapter 2
United States Geography: Physical and Human Systems

This chapter addresses the following Louisiana iLeap standards:

G-1C-M3:	5. Explain patterns of rural/urban migration and the positive and negative consequences of urban development in the United States.
G-1C-M4:	6. Identify selected racial, ethnic, and religious groups that settled in the United States and explain the political, cultural, and economic reasons for immigration.
G-1C-M6:	7. Compare the interdependence of Great Britain and the American colonies to the global economy today.
G-1C-M7:	8. Explain how cooperation and conflict affected the changing political boundaries of the United States to 1877 (e.g., Missouri Compromise).
G-1D-M2	9. Explain how the different physical environments in the American North and South led to different economic activities
E-1A-M9:	41. Use economic concepts (e.g., supply and demand, interdependence) to explain Mercantilism and describe its role in British colonization and the conflict between the thirteen American colonies and Great Britain
E-1B-M6:	42. Identify U.S. exports and imports that contributed to the U.S. economic interdependence with Europe and other parts of the world during the eighteenth and nineteenth centuries

2.1 MIGRATION, IMMIGRATION, AND URBAN DEVELOPMENT

WESTERN MIGRATION

When people move from one part of a country to another, it is called **migration**. Throughout US history, people have **migrated for different reasons**. As we discussed in chapter 1, many people migrated west during the colonial period and the early years of the nation. Some moved west for religious reasons. Many Christian missionaries went to spread the message of Jesus Christ to Native Americans. One group, the Mormons, moved west to escape religious persecution. They founded their own settlement in what is today Utah. Others

Settlers Moving West

traveled west in search of gold. The Gold Rush of 1849 attracted thousands to California and eventually led to statehood for the territory. Later gold rushes increased the population of the Rocky Mountains as well (review chapter 1, section 1.2). Gold ultimately became one of the major reasons for conflict between white settlers and Native Americans. Following the abolition of slavery, many African Americans moved west, hoping to escape southern racism and start a new life. Many African Americans lived as farmers, cowboys, or soldiers in the United States Army.

New York City in the Late 1800s

Available land also drew people west. In 1862, Congress passed laws making it easier for people to own western land. One of these laws was the **Homestead Act**. Under the Homestead Act, those willing to cultivate 160 acres of land for five years were granted ownership. The law helped increase the western population.

URBANIZATION

Factory in the Late 1800s

Blacks in City Around WWI

During the 1800s, the US experienced a period of rapid **urbanization**. Urbanization occurs when cities grow and become central to a country's economy and culture. In the West, new towns grew out of nothing, thanks to mining, farming, cattle ranching, and railroads. Meanwhile, in the East, established cities grew in population due to industrialization. **Industrialization** occurs when a nation's economy comes to rely on modern technology and factories for increased production. As machines took the place of manual labor and assembly lines increased the pace of work, factories and mills became more and more common. Cities became centers of industry. Industrialization transformed US business, made a number of business owners rich, and created new job opportunities. Since rising farm costs and falling agricultural prices meant that fewer people could make a living farming, many people left their farms and migrated to cities where they could earn higher wages. Western cities like San Francisco began to grow and thrive. Denver, Kansas City, and Omaha also transformed from frontier villages into booming urban areas. The South also experienced urbanization thanks to industries like tobacco, iron production, and textiles. However, it was northeastern cities like New York that saw the greatest numbers in population growth. Initially, most migrants to northern cities were white. During World War I, however, a large number of African Americans flocked to northern cities to fill available jobs and improve their standard of living. Historians came to call this period of African American relocation the **Great Migration**.

IMMIGRATION

When people come to a new country from a foreign land, it is called **immigration**. The first European settlers to North America were immigrants. Over the centuries, several waves of mass immigration have occurred in the US. During the mid-1700s, many immigrants came from England, Scotland, Ireland, Germany, and France. Large numbers of them sought religious freedom, such as the Puritans of New England. Others desired land and a chance to make their fortune.

THE ACADIANS

France's first settlement in Canada became home to a group of French settlers known as the **Acadians**. In 1713, France ceded the portion of Canada where the Acadians lived to Great Britain. In 1754, the British government insisted the Acadians swear allegiance to King George II. The Acadians refused because of their French heritage. In response, the British expelled them from Canada in 1755. Some Acadians went to France. Many emigrated to the US. A large number of Acadians made their way to Louisiana, where they became known by a new name: **Cajuns**.

Acadians of the 1700s

Modern Cajun

GERMAN AND IRISH IMMIGRANTS

During the first half of the 1800s, most of the immigrants who arrived in the eastern United States came from Western Europe. Many came to seek jobs created by industrialization. Others came to escape religious or political persecution. Some came to flee droughts, famine, or wars. In the 1840s, a large number of **Germans** fled Europe to escape political conflicts. Many of them settled as farmers in the Midwest. Others settled in northern cities like New York, Chicago, and Milwaukee.

Irish Immigrants

Between 1820 and 1860, almost half the immigrants who came to the US were **Irish**. Many came to escape the Great Irish Potato Famine that occurred between 1845 and 1850. During a famine, people die of starvation because of a lack of food. Others simply sought economic opportunities. Irish immigrants settled in cities like New York, Boston, Philadelphia, and Chicago. Even today, more people of Irish ancestry live in New York City than in Dublin, the capital of Ireland.

CHINESE IMMIGRANTS

Chinese Immigrants in the 1800s

On the west coast, many of the immigrants who arrived came from Eastern Asia. A large number of **Chinese** settled in cities like San Francisco. Along with Irish immigrants, many Chinese arrivals found work building railroads. Most historians (people who study history for a living) agree that western railroads could not have been constructed as quickly as they were without the efforts of immigrants. Unfortunately for the Chinese, many US citizens opposed immigration. They resented immigrants' willingness to work for less money. The cheap labor Chinese immigrants provided drove down wages and meant that foreigners were hired instead of people born in the United States. As railroads were completed and the need for labor decreased, opponents of immigration succeeded in convincing the federal government to pass the **Chinese Exclusion Act of 1882**. The law made it illegal for Chinese people to immigrate to the United States. It was not repealed (canceled) until 1943.

Late Nineteenth Century Immigration

Towards the end of the 1800s, immigration increased again. This time, many of the immigrants who came to the US were from **Eastern and Southern Europe** (nations like Russia, Poland, Greece, and Italy). More **Jewish people** also immigrated to the United States to escape religious persecution. Some of these immigrants were wealthy or intellectuals (highly educated people). Many were very poor. To handle the large numbers of people arriving in the country, the federal government opened **Ellis Island** in 1892. The island rested in New York Harbor, near the Statue of Liberty. It became a well known reception center for immigrants arriving by ship. Wealthier passengers were allowed to disembark and go directly to their destination. Poorer passengers had to be checked for hygiene (bodily cleanliness), contagious diseases, and to see if they had a friend or family member in the US who could help them adjust. The federal government did not want to let anyone into the country who might cause trouble or be unable to take care of themselves. Since many immigrants could not speak English or understand why they were being poked and prodded, Ellis Island often proved to be a confusing and terrifying experience.

Ellis Island

Push and Pull Factors

Push and pull factors contribute to immigration. *Push factors* are those things that push someone out of their own country. Political or religious persecution, natural disasters, or anything else that would make someone want to leave their homeland are all examples of push factors. *Pull factors* are things that attract someone to a new country. Political freedom, job opportunities, or the chance to be reunited with family are a few examples of pull factors. Even today, people immigrate to the United States because of push and pull factors.

Consequences of Urban Development

Positive Consequences

US urbanization had a number of **positive consequences**. Industrialization created jobs that led US citizens to migrate from rural areas to cities. It also inspired record numbers of immigrants to come to the United States. The mass immigration increased the nation's **cultural diversity** (the presence of people from many different cultural and ethnic backgrounds). Immigrants brought different languages, customs, religious beliefs, styles of food and dress, and so on. Such diversity inspired the phrase "melting pot." In a melting pot, people mix different ingredients together as they make a delicious final product. In the same way, many saw the United States as a place where people of all backgrounds could assimilate into

Immigrants Living in a US City
During the Early 1900s

American society. In reality, however, most immigrants did not want to fully assimilate. They wanted to maintain many of their traditions. (Assimilation means to become culturally like most people in a society.)

Migration and immigration caused urban populations to increase dramatically. Industrialization provided new jobs and higher wages than many workers had ever earned before. The demands of growing cities also led to technological advances like electricity. Electricity allowed factories to stay open after dark, increasing industrial production. It also made new products like sewing machines and refrigerators possible. Electronic products made work at home faster, giving people more time for leisure activity. Electric light also meant that people could stay out later. Saloons, restaurants, and nighttime entertainment became common. Trolleys provided public transportation that allowed people to live outside the inner city. New forms of leisure and entertainment arose. Professional sports, Vaudeville shows, motion pictures, and public parks all became popular during the age of rapid urbanization.

Trolley in the Early 20th Century

Professional Baseball in 1920

NEGATIVE CONSEQUENCES

Unfortunately, urbanization had **negative consequences** as well. Cities became overcrowded. Crime increased. Poorer immigrants and citizens often lived in urban slums (poor, inner-city neighborhoods) consisting of tenements (overcrowded apartments that housed several families of immigrants or poor laborers). These slums often had open sewers that attracted rats and other disease-spreading pests. Pollution was another problem. The air was usually dark with soot from coal-fired steam engines and boilers. Meanwhile, the individual tenements were often unclean, full of fire hazards, and occupied by more than one family crammed together into a small apartment. People from different backgrounds and countries tended to live in ethnically divided neighborhoods. These divisions created rivalries and mistrust that led to racism and violence. In some areas, environmental concerns grew as the growing urban population led to more construction and increased deforestation (review chapter 1, section 1.2).

MIGRATION, IMMIGRATION, AND URBANIZATION TODAY

An Urban Tenement

Today, people continue to migrate from one region of the United States to another in search of better jobs and opportunities. For example, in recent years economic changes have led many people in the northeastern United States to migrate to the South and West. Urban areas still attract people because of the abundant jobs and cultural opportunities they offer. Meanwhile, foreign immigrants still come to the US every year. Some come legally. They go through the necessary procedures and abide by federal laws which allow them to enter and remain in the country. Others come illegally, crossing the border without legal permission or remaining after their legal right to stay has expired.

Many US immigrants come from Latin American nations. The Latin American population has grown so rapidly over the last few decades that Hispanics have surpassed African Americans as the largest minority in the United States. Immigration and migration continue to make the United States an ever-changing society that is rich in cultural diversity.

Urban Population Today

Practice 2.1: Migration, Immigration, and Urban Development

1. The Homestead Act contributed to western migration because it helped white settlers acquire

    A. gold.
    B. religious freedom.
    C. land.
    D. jobs.

2. When cities grow in population and become economic and industrial centers of a nation, this process is called

    A. industrialization.
    B. urbanization.
    C. migration.
    D. immigration.

3. Louisiana Cajuns can trace their roots to the
   A. Irish.   B. Germans.   C. Chinese.   D. Acadians.

4. What is migration, and what are some reasons people migrate?

5. What is immigration, and what are some reasons people immigrate?

2.2 GEOGRAPHICAL IMPACT: ECONOMICALLY AND POLITICALLY

ECONOMIC IMPACT

Colonial Trade

Geography impacts people economically and politically. As more and more European settlers arrived in North America, the colonies and Europe developed an **economic interdependence** (depended on one another economically). The colonies produced raw materials like lumber, tobacco, cotton, sugarcane, and so on. They shipped these materials to Europe. European manufacturers then used them to produce goods they sold to the colonies. Europe depended on the colonies for cheap resources, and the colonies depended on Europe for finished goods.

One of the major reasons European nations like france and Great Britain established colonies was **mercantilism**. Mercantilism was the belief that nations needed to export more goods than they imported. Colonies were valuable because they provided countries with more resources and markets for finished goods.

IMPACT OF ENVIRONMENT

The **environment** also played a key role in economic development. In the South, the climate and soil proved suitable for growing crops like rice, tobacco, sugarcane, and cotton. Because people in Europe and elsewhere demanded these agricultural products, such crops became the basis of the South's economy. Meanwhile, the thick forests of the Carolinas and Georgia provided turpentine and tar, which were necessary naval stores (materials for shipbuilding). The environment also prevented large cities from developing in the South. Due to the region's many rivers and tributaries, ships could often travel further inland and pick up cargo directly from southern plantations (large farms that raised cash crops). As a result, southern landowners did not have to rely on large port cities to ship their goods overseas. Further north, however, where ships had less inland acess, cities like New York, Philadelphia, and Boston became key centers of trade. These urban centers provided harbors for ships departing with raw materials and arriving with finished goods.

The North had a different economy from the South. Although there were northern farmers, they tended to grow things like wheat and corn rather than cotton, tobacco, or sugar. Meanwhile, craftsmen's shops, banks, merchants, taverns, printing shops, and many other businesses arose in urban areas. Therefore, the North came to rely much more on business and commerce than did the South. In New England, much of the farming was subsistence (only enough to provide what local residents needed).

Northern Industry in the 1800s

Shipbuilding and fishing became major industries in northern cities along the Atlantic coast.

GEOGRAPHY'S IMPACT ON POLITICAL BOUNDARIES

SLAVERY

US Slavery

Geography affects political boundaries. As the South grew more dependent on cash crops and the North became more centered around business and manufacturing, serious tensions arose. Since 1619, **slavery** had existed in the United States. Following the American Revolution, however, many leaders began to call for its abolishment (end). Northern states were not nearly as dependent on slavery and claimed that it violated the principles of the Declaration of Independence. Southern states were divided. States in the Upper South (Virginia and Maryland) wanted to keep slavery but end the Atlantic slave trade (process of shipping slaves from Africa for sale in the US). Their regions already had a high number of slaves. They feared too many slaves could lead to a slave rebellion. They also believed that ending the Atlantic slave trade would allow them to make money by establishing a domestic (US) slave trade. This domestic slave trade would involve selling slaves from the Upper South to the Deep South and western territories. States in the Deep South wanted to keep slavery and the Atlantic slave trade. Only a series of political compromises between the different regions kept the peace. Leaders agreed to outlaw slavery in the Northwest Territory north of the Ohio River (see chapter 1, section 1.2). In return, slavery continued in the southern region that became Alabama and Mississippi. For a time, political tensions subsided.

THE LOUISIANA PURCHASE

Thomas Jefferson

As the US population grew, so did the need for land and resources. Following the American Revolution, the United States was a young nation that was economically dependent on Europe. The nation's third president, Thomas Jefferson, recognized that the land west of the Mississippi River offered valuable resources that would help the United States be more self-sufficient (able to take care of itself). The **Louisiana Purchase** of 1803 roughly doubled the size of the country and gave the US valuable land between the Mississippi River and the Rocky Mountains.

THE MISSOURI COMPROMISE

The Louisiana Purchase reignited the slavery debate. Earlier compromises only settled the slavery issue east of the Mississippi River. Now political leaders had to decide whether or not to allow slavery in the new western territories. Northern leaders opposed allowing slavery west of the Mississippi River. Many northern states had already outlawed slavery. Some northern leaders opposed slavery because they thought it was immoral. Others felt it gave the South an unfair economic and political advantage. Slaves provided southerners with free labor the North did not have and more slave states would increase the number of leaders who supported the institution. Southern political leaders favored slavery in the new territory. They knew that regions of the Louisiana Territory would eventually become states. If these states did not have slavery, they would likely vote against the South's interests in Congress. The conflict came to a head in 1819. Citizens of Missouri applied for statehood. Slave states and free states were equally represented in the Senate, and Missouri's admission would change the balance of power. Senator Jesse B. Thomas of Illinois proposed a bill calling for the admission of Missouri as a slave state and Maine as a free state. In addition, the southern boundary of Missouri would become a dividing line for any new states admitted to the Union. All new states north of that line would be free states, while those to the south would be slave states. Congress passed the bill and President Monroe signed it into law in 1820. It became known as the **Missouri Compromise**.

The Missouri Compromise

LAND FROM MEXICO

During the 1800s, many people in the United States adopted the idea of **Manifest Destiny**. Those who believed in Manifest Destiny felt that it was the United States' destiny to conquer and control all the territory between Mexico and Canada from the Atlantic to the Pacific Ocean. In 1844, James K. Polk became president of the United States. He believed in Manifest Destiny. In 1846, he led the United States into a war with Mexico in an effort to gain more territory. After a series of US victories, Mexico finally surrendered. The two sides signed the **Treaty of Guadalupe-Hidalgo** in 1848. The treaty required Mexico to sell the New Mexico and California territories to the United States. As the US economy continued to grow and the federal government wanted to build more western railroads, President Franklin Pierce sent James Gadsden to buy more land from Mexico. The **Gadsden Purchase** gave the United States parts of present-day New Mexico and Arizona.

James K Polk

Land Acquired in the Treaty of Guadalupe-Hidalgo and Gadsden Purchase

RECAP OF GEOGRAPHY'S POLITICAL AND ECONOMIC INFLUENCE

Geographic features affect regions economically. In the South, climate, soil, and available water routes created an agricultural society that grew to rely heavily on slave labor. In the North, access to the Atlantic Ocean, fewer inland water routes, and different climate and soil from that found in the South created an economy dependent on commerce, fishing, shipbuilding, and different agricultural products. Where forests were abundant, US regions depended on naval stores and lumber. Economic concerns affect politics. Political leaders seek to protect the economic well-being of their regions. Southern leaders sought to protect slavery

United States Geography: Physical and Human Systems

because it was a key part of their agricultural economy. The federal government wanted to expand territory in order to gain more resources that would make the nation wealthier. Throughout US history, geographical features have affected economics and politics.

Practice 2.2: Geographical Impact: Economically and Politically

1. A farmer in South Carolina raises indigo. He then ships his product overseas to Europe. European manufacturers use the indigo to make clothes, which they ship back to be sold in the colonies. This is an example of

   A. politics.

   B. environmental concerns.

   C. economic interdependence.

   D. slavery.

2. How did geography affect the economies of the North and South?

3. Why did political leaders come up with the Missouri Compromise?

CHAPTER 2 REVIEW

Key Terms, People, and Concepts

migration	Ellis Island
reasons people migrate	push/pull factors
urbanization	positive consequences of urbanization
industrialization	cultural diversity
Great Migration	negative consequences of urbanization
immigration	migration, immigration, urbanization today
Acadians	economic interdependence
Cajuns	mercantilism
German immigrants	environment's impact on economy/politics
Irish immigrants	Louisiana Purchase
Chinese immigrants	slavery
Chinese Exclusion Act of 1882	Missouri Compromise
Eastern and Southern European immigrants	Manifest Destiny
Jewish immigrants	Treaty of Guadalupe-Hidalgo
	Gadsden Purchase

Multiple Choice Questions

Chapter 2

1. During the eighteenth and nineteenth centuries, many people in the United States migrated west in search of

   A. urbanization.
   B. immigrants.
   C. land and gold.
   D. political debate.

2. Martin GeBeaux has lived in southwest Louisiana his entire life. He speaks English, but people who hear him talk can detect a slight accent that stems from his French heritage. Martin is most likely a/an

   A. Irish immigrant.
   B. Cajun descendant of Acadians.
   C. French Canadian.
   D. Acadian immigrant.

3. African Americans moving to the western United States after the Civil War and to northern cities during World War I are examples of

   A. urbanization.   B. migration.   C. immigration.   D. abolition.

4. Which of the following had the LEAST impact on migration and immigration?

   A. industrialization
   B. the Homestead Act
   C. religious persecutions
   D. shipbuilding

5. The Great Irish Potato Famine of the 1840s led many Irish citizens to flee their homeland for the US. The famine was an example of a

   A. push factor.
   B. pull factor.
   C. political factor.
   D. cultural diversity.

6. Urban slums, overcrowding, increased crime, and pollution were all

   A. reasons for cultural diversity.
   B. pull factors for immigration.
   C. negative consequences of urbanization.
   D. positive consequences of immigration.

7. The South's dependence on cash crops like sugarcane and cotton is an example of

   A. how environment affects economy.
   B. slavery.
   C. political debates.
   D. how geography determines migration.

8. Which of the following dealt most directly with the issue of slavery?

   A. Louisiana Purchase
   B. Missouri Compromise
   C. Gadsden Purchase
   D. Treaty of Guadalupe-Hidalgo

Chapter 3
United States Government

This chapter addresses the following Louisiana iLeap standards:

C-1A-M1:	10. Explain and evaluate the major purposes of government
C-1A-M2:	11. Explain the meaning of the term *federalism*
	12. Distinguish between various forms of government (e.g., monarchy, totalitarian) and describe their characteristics and organization
C-1A-M3:	13. Explain how separation of powers limits government and describe the U.S. government system of checks and balances
	14. Identify the powers of the U.S. federal government and the powers it shares with state governments according to the U.S. Constitution
C-1A-M5:	15. Identify the structure and powers of the three branches of the federal government, the limits of those powers, and key positions within each branch
C-1A-M6:	16. Identify qualifications and terms of office for elected officials at the national level
	17. Identify current government leaders at the national level
	18. Describe the powers/responsibilities and limits of power for government officials at the national level
C-1A-M7:	19. Explain how a bill becomes law at the federal level
	20. Examine a given law or court ruling and evaluate it based on given criteria (e.g., Dred Scott decision)
C-1A-M10:	21. Evaluate a type of tax in an historical context (e.g., Stamp Act, Tea Tax)

3.1 PURPOSE AND STRUCTURE OF US GOVERNMENT

TYPES OF GOVERNMENTS

Governments provide structure and order. Different types of governments exist from country to country. Many nations have changed their structure of government over time. A **direct democracy** allows citizens to vote on issues and elect leaders directly. A **republic** is similar to a democracy. It also allows people to have a voice in their government. However, in a republic voting rights are usually restricted, and the people elect representatives who choose executives, make laws, and govern on their behalf. Often, these leaders come from an "elite" ruling class. Under the US Constitution (the national body of laws that

Direct Democracy

establishes the structure and power of US government), the United States government was founded as a republic. People elected members to the House of Representatives directly. However, members of the Senate and delegates who elected the US president were chosen by state legislatures. During the nineteenth and twentieth centuries, the electoral process shifted toward democracy. Citizens began demanding a more direct say in their government. Today, the people directly elect members of both houses of Congress and the president. Such changes illustrate the basic difference between a republic and a direct democracy.

Queen Elizabeth II
(Monarch)

Adolf Hitler
(Totalitarian Dictator)

There are many other forms of government as well. An **autocracy** places power in the hands of a single person, such as an emperor or king. A king or queen with unlimited power rules an **absolute monarchy**. A **constitutional monarchy** limits a king's or queen's power by requiring them to abide by a constitution (a set of national laws). In a constitutional monarchy, the monarch usually shares power with another branch of government, such as a parliament. Under a **dictatorship**, a single ruler or political party rules with no restrictions on power. Many times, a dictatorship is an autocracy, because the dictator is a single individual. However, a collective body can also form a dictatorship. Many dictatorships are totalitarian. **Totalitarian governments** insist that the state is far more important than individuals. Nearly every aspect of society is controlled by the government, and political opposition is not permitted. Personal rights mean very little in a totalitarian government. An **oligarchy** is a government in which power is in the hands of a small group of people, usually from the upper class. A **theocracy** bases government on religion. The Taliban government, which the US overthrew in Afghanistan as part of its war on terror, was an example of a theocracy. It was based on an interpretation of Muslim law.

PURPOSES OF US GOVERNMENT

The **United States Constitution** establishes the laws limiting and empowering the United States government. Its opening sentence, called the *Preamble*, defines the purpose of the national government.

> *"We the people of the United States, in order to form a more perfect union, establish justice, insure domestic tranquility, provide for the common defense, promote the general welfare, and secure the blessings of liberty to ourselves and our posterity, do ordain and establish this Constitution for the United States of America."*

Constitutional Convention

According to the Preamble, the United States government was established to:

1. **insure domestic tranquility:** The US government maintains peace and order.

2. **provide for the common defense:** The government is responsible for protecting US citizens from outside dangers and enemies that might attack the United States.

3. **promote the general welfare:** The government is meant to pass laws and enact policies that better the lives of citizens and improve US society.

US Capitol Building

4. **secure the blessings of liberty:** The United States government is charged with protecting the liberties of US citizens both now and for generations to come.

5. **make laws:** In order to carry out its function, the US government is empowered by the Constitution to make and enforce laws that govern the country and establish justice.

FEDERALISM

A key principle of the United States government is **federalism**. In a federalist system, two levels of government share power. In the United States, the national and state governments each have authority over certain areas. According to the Constitution's Tenth Amendment, those powers that are not restricted by the Constitution nor delegated to the national government are reserved for the states. Powers delegated solely to the national government are called **delegated powers**. Powers reserved for the states are called **reserved powers**. Powers exercised by both levels of government are called **concurrent powers**.

Examples of Delegated Powers

- print money
- establish a post office
- negotiate and approve treaties with foreign nations
- declare war
- raise an army

Delegated Powers

Examples of Reserved Powers

- establish school systems
- organize and conduct elections
- establish counties, municipalities, and guidelines for local governments

Reserved Powers

Examples of Concurrent Powers

- pass and enforce laws
- tax citizens
- establish courts

CHECKS AND BALANCES

Congressional Debate

Three branches make up the federal government. The **legislative branch** makes the nation's laws; the **executive branch** enforces the laws; and the **judicial branch** makes sure that all laws and the manner in which they are enforced are constitutional. We will examine the roles and powers of these branches more in section 3.2.

A system of **checks and balances** prevents any one branch from becoming too powerful. Although one branch might enjoy a certain power, another branch can still "check" or "balance" its power if need be. For example, Congress has the power to pass bills it believes should become law. The president, however, has the authority to "check" this power by vetoing (rejecting) any bill Congress passes. A **presidential veto** prevents a bill from becoming a law. However, if Congress has enough votes, it can **override** a veto (vote to ignore the president's rejection of the bill). It takes two-thirds of the representatives in the House and

President Bush Signing a new Law

two-thirds of the senators in the Senate to override a veto. If an override occurs, the bill becomes law. This is just one example of how checks and balances work. Below are some other examples.

- **Judicial Review:** Judicial review occurs when the federal courts review a law passed by Congress to determine if it is constitutional (allowed under the US Constitution). If the courts rule the law is unconstitutional, then the law no longer applies. The courts can also pass rulings on whether or not the president is acting within the rules of the Constitution when he or she enforces a law.

Judicial Review

- **Judicial Appointments:** The president and Congress both have checks over the courts as well. The president appoints judges to serve in the judicial branch. The United States Senate must approve these appointments.

- **Presidential Nominees:** The president has the power to appoint individuals to certain positions. For instance, the president appoints members of the cabinet, heads of certain agencies, and ambassadors to other countries. Before these individuals may take office, however, the United States Senate must approve them.

- **Ratification of treaties:** The Constitution grants the president the power to negotiate and sign treaties with foreign nations. However, before they become official and binding on the United States, the Senate must ratify (approve) them.

Congressional Hearing

- **Impeachment:** Impeachment is, perhaps, the most drastic example of checks and balances. Under the Constitution, the House of Representatives has the power to impeach (charge with wrongdoing while in office) public officials, including the president of the United States. If two-thirds of the Senate agrees that the impeached official is guilty, then that person is removed from office. Only two US presidents have been impeached: Andrew Johnson (1868) and Bill Clinton (1998). The Senate acquitted (found "not guilty") both presidents.

Clinton During the Impeachment Process

Practice 3.1: Purpose and Structure of US Government

1. A form of government in which citizens vote directly to elect leaders and settle public issues is
   A. direct democracy.
   B. republicanism.
   C. federalism.
   D. autocracy.

2. Under the Constitution, the United States was originally established as a
   A. direct democracy.
   B. republic.
   C. dictatorship.
   D. theocracy.

3. According to the Preamble to the Constitution, which of the following is a role of government?
   A. federalism
   B. reserving powers
   C. securing the blessings of liberty
   D. preventing domestic tranquility

4. What is federalism? How does federalism work in the United States?

5. Define checks and balances and give an example of how this process works in US government.

3.2 SEPARATION OF POWERS

THE LEGISLATIVE BRANCH – CONGRESS

Separation of powers prevents any one branch of US government from becoming too powerful. The **legislative branch** consists of Congress and is responsible for making the nation's laws. Congress includes two houses: the House of Representatives and the United States Senate. Population determines how many representatives each state has in the **House of Representatives**. The greater a state's population, the more representatives that state has. Voters elect representatives to the House every two years. Once in office, these representatives elect the **speaker of the House** (usually from the majority party) to serve as the House of Representatives' leader.

Speaker of the House Nancy Pelosi

President Pro Tempore Robert Byrd

The **Senate** is comprised of two senators from each state. Originally, state legislatures elected senators. However, in 1913, the Seventeenth Amendment to the Constitution changed this. Now, citizens directly elect US senators who serve six-year terms. The senator who has represented a particular state the longest is called the *senior senator*. The senator who has served less time is called the *junior senator*. The vice president presides over the Senate. However, a **president pro tempore** leads the Senate when the vice president is absent. The president pro tempore is the highest ranking senator. The most senior member of the majority party usually serves in this position.

Each main party (Democrats and Republicans) also has majority and minority leaders in each house. The **Senate majority leader** is the lead senator for the party with the majority (more than half) of seats in the Senate. The **Senate minority leader** is the lead senator for the party with a minority of seats (less than half). In the same way, the **House majority leader** is the lead representative for the party with the majority of seats in the House of Representatives, and the **House minority leader** is the lead representative for the party with a minority of seats. These leaders try to ensure that Congress acts in ways that are in the best interest of their particular political parties.

Vice President Joe Biden

POWERS AND LIMITATIONS OF CONGRESS

The Constitution grants each house of Congress certain powers and responsibilities. Some powers are shared by both houses. Others belong to one house but not the other. For instance, both houses must approve a bill before it can become a law. On the other hand, only the House of Representatives may introduce tax bills or impeach public officials, and only the Senate has the power to block or confirm presidential appointments and ratify treaties. The following graphs describe some of the powers and limitations of Congress.

Congress has the power to *impeach* (charge with wrongdoing while in office) public officials.
Congress can try impeachment cases and decide the guilt or innocence of impeached public officials.
Congress must confirm (accept) or reject presidential appointments.
Congress can ratify or reject treaties with foreign nations.
Congress has the power to propose taxes and means of raising revenue.
Only Congress may introduce bills and pass new laws and/or resolutions.
Congress may borrow money and regulate foreign and interstate trade.
Congress has the authority to coin money, establish rules by which foreign immigrants become citizens, establish bankruptcy laws, post offices, and provide copyrights and patents protecting artists and inventors.
Only Congress may declare war on behalf of the United States.
It is up to Congress to provide money for maintaining a national military force.

Congress cannot suspend *writ of habeas corpus*. This is the right of an arrested person to go before a judge within a reasonable amount of time to determine if their incarceration is justified. Congress may not suspend this right except in cases of rebellion, invasion, or to ensure public safety.
Congress may not pass "bills of attainder" (legislative acts convicting people of crimes without a trial).
Congress may not establish *ex post facto* laws (laws that make some past activity illegal, even though it was not illegal at the time). For instance, if the government established a law making profanity on television illegal, it could not prosecute people for using profanity on TV prior to the law being passed.
Congress may not grant "titles of nobility." Sorry, but no matter what you do, Congress cannot name you the *Duke* or *Duchess of Louisiana*.
Congress is limited in what kinds of taxes and duties it may establish and how it may govern trade.

Qualifications to Serve in Congress			
House	Minimum Age	Citizenship Requirements	Term Length
House of Representatives	25 years	US citizen at least 7 years and a resident of the state one represents at the time of election.	2 years
US Senate	30 years	US citizen at least 9 years and a resident of the state one represents at the time of election.	6 years

THE EXECUTIVE BRANCH — THE PRESIDENT, VICE PRESIDENT, AND CABINET

The **executive branch** enforces the laws. The **president of the United States** serves as the chief executive of this branch and the nation's head of state (leader). Under the Constitution, the president is elected to office by the **Electoral College**. This is a body of delegates that meets every four years to elect the president and the **vice president**. Each state's delegation in the Electoral College equals its number of representatives and senators in Congress. Today, this body serves as a formality since delegates' votes are predetermined in a general election.

President Obama

Once elected, the president and vice president are then inaugurated (swear an oath to uphold the duties of their respective offices). They serve four-year terms. Although the Constitution did not originally place limits on how many terms a president may serve, none served more than two terms until 1940. That year, Franklin Delano

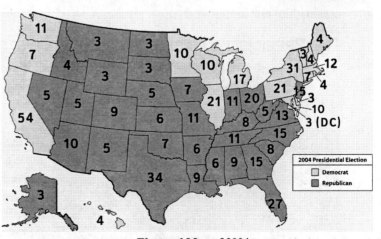

Electoral Map of 2004

Roosevelt broke tradition and became the only president in history elected to a third term (he was eventually elected four times). Later, in 1951, the Twenty-second Amendment limited presidents to no more than two terms.

RESPONSIBILITIES AND POWERS OF THE PRESIDENT AND VICE PRESIDENT

The Constitution lists the qualifications for president and defines his or her powers and responsibilities.

The president is to serve as commander in chief of the nation's military. In other words, he or she is the top military commander.
The president represents the US and is responsible for negotiating treaties with other nations (treaties must be ratified by the Senate before they are official).
The president appoints public officials, such as heads of federal departments and federal judges.
The president is the head of the executive branch and is responsible for enforcing federal laws.

President George W. Bush with a World Leader

Under the Constitution, the president may be **impeached** by the House of Representatives if he or she is suspected of treason, bribery, or "other high crimes and misdemeanors." If this occurs, the president then stands trial in the Senate. If two-thirds of the Senate finds him or her guilty, the president is removed from office.

The vice president is also part of the executive branch and presides over the Senate. The vice president has no vote in the Senate, however, unless there is a tie. In that case, the vice-president casts the tie-breaking vote. If the president cannot fulfill a full term in office, the vice president becomes president until the next presidential election.

THE PRESIDENT'S CABINET AND JOINT CHIEFS OF STAFF

President George W. Bush and his Presidential Cabinet

One part of the executive branch that is not established by the Constitution is the **president's cabinet**. The cabinet evolved over time and consists of the heads of various federal departments. Its members serve as the president's official advisors and representatives. The secretary of state advises the president on foreign affairs and often acts as the president's representative to foreign governments. The secretary of defense is in charge of the military. The attorney general is the nation's top law enforcement official and is over agencies like the FBI. These are just a few examples of officials who serve on the president's cabinet. They are appointed by the president and must be approved by the Senate. Usually, they serve until the president who appointed them leaves office.

As commander in chief, the president also depends on advice from the **Joint Chiefs of Staff**. The Joint Chiefs of Staff consists of commanding officers from each major branch of the United States military. These commanders provide the president with expertise and advice regarding matters involving the armed forces.

Secretary of State Hillary Clinton

Chairman of the Joint Chiefs of Staff
Admiral Michael G. Mullen

Qualifications for President and Vice President			
Office	Minimum Age	Citizenship Requirements	Term Length
President	35 years	Must be a natural-born citizen and have lived in the US at least 14 years.	4 years
Vice President	Same as the president	Same as the president	Same as the president

The Judicial Branch – The Federal Courts

Current US Supreme Court

The **judicial branch** consists of the federal court system, with the **US Supreme Court** serving as the highest court in the land. The role of the judicial branch is to make sure that laws are constitutional and applied appropriately. Unlike the president, vice president, and members of the legislative branch, judges who serve in the judicial branch are not elected. Rather, they are **appointed** (given their position) by the president for life. The reason they are appointed is so they will be free to make decisions based on law, without having to worry about political pressures. The Supreme Court consists of nine judges, called *justices*. One justice serves as the **chief justice** (lead justice) while the other eight serve as **associate justices**. These justices have appellate jurisdiction (the authority to review the decisions of lower courts) over all federal and state court cases. The Supreme Court also has original jurisdiction (authority to hear a case first) over, "cases affecting ambassadors, other public ministers and consuls, and those in which a state shall be a party." Underneath the Supreme Court are lower federal courts.

Former Supreme Court Chief Justice John Marshall

Current Chief Justice John G Roberts, Jr

One of the most important powers of the judicial branch is not specifically granted by the Constitution. Insted, it was established by precedence in 1803. **Precedence** means a court uses past legal decisions to make rulings because the law is open to interpretation or there is no written statute. In 1801, Thomas Jefferson (an Anti-federalist) became president. However, just before leaving office, his predecessor, John Adams (a Federalist), appointed a number of federal judges. Although the Senate had confirmed these judges and Adams had signed their appointments, the documents making their appointments official had not yet been delivered when Jefferson took office. Fearing that Federalist judges might interfere with his plans, Jefferson refused to deliver the documents, preventing some of the judges from ever taking office. When several of the appointees challenged this move, the Supreme Court head the case. In *Marbury v. Madison (1803)*, Chief Justice John Marshall stated that the appointees were entitled to their commissions *but* that the US Supreme Court did not have authority under the Constitution to force the president to issue them. Marshall's decision struck down part of a federal law giving the Court such authority and established **judicial review.** The case made it clear that federal courts can declare acts of Congress unconstitutional.

Practice 3.2: Separation of Powers

1. Congress is responsible for
   A. military policy.
   B. foreign negotiations.
   C. making laws.
   D. court decisions.

2. Members of the president's cabinet are part of the
   A. judicial branch.
   B. executive branch.
   C. legislative branch.
   D. Joint Chiefs of Staff.

3. Angela is an elected official in the federal government. She is one of ten people representing her state and about to finish her third two-year term. Angela is
   A. an official in the executive branch of government.
   B. a United States senator.
   C. a United States representative.
   D. a federal judge.

4. List some of the powers given to Congress under the Constitution. What are some of the limitations placed on Congress?

5. What are some of the major roles of the president of the United States?

3.3 How a Bill Becomes Law

Legislative Process

US Capitol Building

The White House

A **bill** (proposed law) must first be introduced in either the House of Representatives or the US Senate. Under the guidelines of the Constitution, both houses vote on the bill. If a majority approves the bill in both houses, then it goes to the president. If the president signs it, the bill becomes a law. If the president vetoes it, the bill goes back to Congress. If two-thirds of the members of each house vote in favor of the bill again, the president's veto is overridden and the bill becomes law anyway. If less than two-thirds in either house vote for the bill, then the bill dies and does not become a law.

Committees and Filibusters

Congressional Committee

A legislative process by which bills make their way through Congress has evolved over time. Although not required by the Constitution, it has become an important part of the federal government. A key part of this process is the role of **committees**. These are panels within each house of Congress that are responsible for studying bills and recommending whether or not they should pass. Once a bill makes it out of committee, it goes before the entire house for debate and a vote. The House of Representatives puts limits on how much time can be spent debating a bill. In the Senate, however, no such limits exist. Senators will sometimes use a **filibuster** to stop a vote on a bill. This is a strategy in which a senator will continue to talk until either the bill is withdrawn, or other senators can convince colleagues to vote "no." If, however, three-fifths of the senators present vote in favor of closing the debate, then the filibuster is ended, and a vote can occur.

Chapter 3

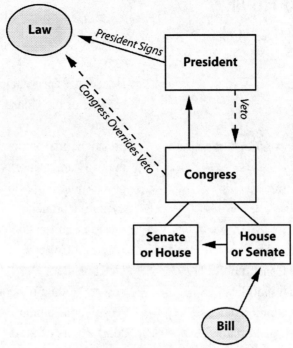

How a Bill Becomes a Law

Practice 3.3: How a Bill Becomes a Law

1. Before the president can sign a bill into law, the Constitution requires that it

   A. make it out of congressional committee.

   B. pass both houses of Congress.

   C. get a two-thirds vote in each house of Congress.

   D. be considered by a committee.

2. Fred really wants a bill to become law. However, he has just received word that the president has rejected it. In order for the bill to still become law, Fred will need

   A. support from two-thirds of both houses.

   B. a veto.

   C. a filibuster.

   D. a committee to recommend that the bill pass.

CHAPTER 3 REVIEW

Key Terms, People, and Concepts

direct democracy
republic
autocracy
absolute and constitutional monarchy
dictatorship
totalitarian government
oligarchy
theocracy
United States Constitution
Preamble to the Constitution
insure domestic tranquility
provide for the common defense
promote the general welfare
secure the blessings of liberty
make laws
federalism
delegated, reserved, and concurrent powers
checks and balances
presidential veto
override
judicial review
presidential appointment process
impeachment
legislative branch

House of Representatives
speaker of the House
Senate
president pro tempore
majority and minority leaders
powers and limitations of Congress
executive branch
president of the United States
Electoral College
vice president
powers of the president
president's cabinet
Joint Chiefs of Staff
judicial branch
US Supreme Court
judicial appointments
justices
chief justice
associate justices
federal and appellate judges
bill
committees
filibuster

Multiple Choice Questions

1. Bernadette is a queen who enjoys total power. She does not have to deal with other branches of government, and she is constrained by no laws. Bernadette rules a/an

    A. constitutional monarchy.
    B. absolute monarchy.
    C. oligarchy.
    D. republic.

2. Eventually, the citizens in Bernadette's country get tired of her and decide to rebel. They remove her from power and replace her with a group of elites who, on behalf of the people, choose a new president and elect a council to rule over the country. They decide that every three years citizens may vote to select which elites may elect leaders to run the government. It sounds like Bernadette has been replaced by a/an

   A. autocracy.
   B. direct democracy.
   C. totalitarian government.
   D. republic.

> "I cannot accept the president's nomination of this candidate. While she is truly a great American, I believe she lacks the qualifications to serve as secretary of defense, and I must vote against her."

3. The statement above was most likely made by

   A. the vice president.
   B. a member of the president's cabinet.
   C. a US Senator.
   D. a member of the House of Representatives.

4. Look at the diagram below. Where should the next arrow be drawn?

Legislative Process Showing a Bill That Becomes Law

   A. from the Senate back to the House
   B. from Congress to the president
   C. from the president to the US Supreme Court
   D. from Congress to the US Supreme Court

5. The president of the United States is head of the
   A. legislative branch.
   B. executive branch.
   C. judicial branch.
   D. Supreme Court.

6. When a president is impeached it means that
   A. he or she is removed from office.
   B. he or she is charged with wrongdoing by the Supreme Court.
   C. his or her treaties are not ratified by Congress.
   D. the Senate must decide if he or she is guilty of a crime.

Look at the political cartoon below.

7. The cartoon most likely deals with
   A. presidential vetos.
   B. impeachment.
   C. federalism.
   D. judicial review.

Chapter 4
The United States Political System

This chapter addresses the following Louisiana iLeap standards:

C-1B-M1:	22. Identify problems the United States faced after the American Revolution that led to the writing of the U.S. Constitution
	23. Compare and contrast the Articles of Confederation with the U.S. Constitution
	24. Identify the roles of the Continental Congress and the Great Compromise in forming the American constitutional government and the federal union
	25. Identify the arguments of the Federalists and Anti-Federalists
	26. Explain how historical English documents, such as the Magna Carta and the English Bill of Rights, influenced American democracy
	27. Explain how ancient governments influenced American democracy and culture
C-1B-M2:	28. Describe historical experiences and factors that defined, influenced, and helped shape American political culture
C-1B-M3:	29. Define and explain the ideas expressed in the Mayflower Compact and the Declaration of Independence
	30. Explain the principles of government embodied in the U.S. Constitution
C-1B-M4:	31. Analyze methods used to institute change or resolve social conflict in U.S. history (e.g., War of 1812, states' rights theory)
C-1B-M5:	32. Explain how changes are made in a democratic society
C-1B-M6:	33. Describe the role of political parties in the American political system
C-1C-M1:	34. Describe political divisions of the world (nation-states)
	35. Explain various processes/strategies nations use to interact
C-1C-M2:	36. Explain how U.S. foreign policy is formed and carried out
C-1C-M3:	37. Identify types of foreign policy issues with reference to current and historical examples (e.g., Middle East conflicts)
C-1D-M1:	38. Identify the qualifications or requirements for U.S. citizenship, including naturalization
C-1D-M2:	39. Explain the importance of various rights and responsibilities of citizenship to the individual or to society at large (e.g., Bill of Rights)
C-1D-M3:	40. Explain issues involving rights and responsibilities of individuals in American society (e.g., rights of individuals with disabilities, responsibility to pay taxes)

4.1 FOUNDATIONS OF US POLITICS

DRAFTING AND RATIFICATION OF THE UNITED STATES CONSTITUTION

ARTICLES OF CONFEDERATION AND SHAYS' REBELLION

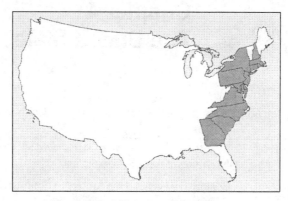

The Original Thirteen Colonies

After declaring independence, the American states did not want to give too much power to a national government. They preferred a confederation. A confederation is a form of government in which the states maintain a great deal of independence while being loosely unified as a nation. For this reason, the **Second Continental Congress** (legislative body that declared independence on July 4, 1776) adopted the **Articles of Confederation**. Finally ratified (approved) in 1781, this document failed because it did not give enough power to the federal (national) government. In order for any law passed by Congress to be final, at least nine of the thirteen states had to agree. Since the states often had different interests, such agreement was rare. Also, the Articles did not grant Congress the power to impose taxes. The federal government had to ask the states for money. This was not very effective and made it impossible to administer the government and provide for a national defense.

Shays' Rebellion

Change finally came after **Shays' Rebellion** in 1786. Following the revolution, the United States experienced an economic crisis. The value of US currency was very low. Falling farm prices left many farmers unable to repay loans. At the same time, in order to pay war debts, the state of Massachusetts raised taxes (the national government could not impose taxes, but state governments could). Outraged, a Massachusetts farmer and Revolutionary War veteran named Daniel Shays led farmers in a rebellion. Without a strong national government, Massachusetts was forced to deal with the revolt on its own. Shays' rebellion made it clear that a more powerful central government was needed to deal with the nation's problems. In 1787, leaders called a convention to revise the Articles of Confederation.

THE CONSTITUTIONAL CONVENTION

When delegates met for their convention, they decided to do away with the Articles of Confederation and write a new set of laws. All the delegates in attendance (only Rhode Island did not send representatives) agreed that change was necessary. However, how the national government should be reorganized was a matter of much debate. As a result, a number of compromises emerged. A **compromise** is an agreement reached when two parties who disagree with one another each gives up a little to come to a conclusion both sides can live with. Because delegates often disagreed, compromise proved crucial at the Constitutional Convention.

Constitutional Convention

Edmund Randolph and James Madison of Virginia introduced the **Virginia Plan**. It called for a federal government made up of three branches: a legislative branch to make the laws; an executive branch to enforce the laws; and a judicial branch to make sure that the laws were fair and properly enforced. The Virginia Plan included a two-house legislature consisting of representatives from each state. In each house, the greater a state's population, the more representatives it would have. Larger states loved the idea; but smaller states hated it because they would have fewer representatives. As a result, one of New Jersey's delegates proposed the **New Jersey Plan**. It also called for three branches of government. However, the legislative branch would have only one house with each state getting a single vote. In the end, the delegates decided to follow a plan that became known as the **Great Compromise.** It was also called the

**Father of the Constitution
James Madison**

Connecticut Plan because it was presented by a delegate from Connecticut. Under this plan, the legislative branch would have two houses. One house, called the House of Representatives, would be elected directly by the people. Each state would be represented according to population. The other house, called the Senate, would be elected by state legislatures. Each state would have two senators, regardless of population. Together, the two houses would comprise Congress.

Slavery also proved to be a point of debate. Northern states had fewer slaves and argued that slaves should not count as part of the population. Southern states, however, had far more slaves and wanted to count them. The answer to this question was important because it affected how many representatives each state would have in Congress. Again, delegates reached a compromise. The **Three-fifths Compromise** stated that each slave would count as "three-fifths of a person." Meanwhile, debate about the slave trade resulted in a **slave trade compromise**. Under this agreement, Northerners and delegates from the Upper South (Maryland and Virginia) who opposed the slave trade agreed to allow it to continue for twenty more years. This was important to delegates from the Deep South who insisted that their economy could not

Slave Trade

survive without the slave trade. Finally, after much debate, the convention presented a new set of national laws to the states for ratification: the **United States Constitution**.

RATIFICATION

Not everyone was pleased with the Constitution. A number of states refused to ratify it, claiming it did not do enough to guarantee the rights of citizens. Finally, in late 1788, the last of the nine states needed for ratification approved the Constitution. They agreed to support the document after Congress promised to consider a number of amendments protecting civil liberties. Only North Carolina and Rhode Island refused to ratify until after these amendments had actually been submitted to Congress. When Congress met in 1789, one of its first acts was to pass ten amendments (additions to the Constitution) that became known as the **Bill of Rights**. These amendments serve to protect the rights of citizens and limit the powers of government.

FEDERALISTS VS. ANTI-FEDERALISTS

Federalist Leaders

Many US citizens favored the Constitution because they believed that the United States needed a strong federal government. Others opposed the Constitution because they feared that a powerful federal government would trample on their rights. Because of the debate, political leaders split into opposing factions. A faction is a group of people who are bound by a common cause, usually against another group bound by an opposing cause. The **Federalists** favored a strong central government and supported the Constitution. Alexander Hamilton, John Adams, and James Madison were among the Federalists' leaders. Federalists also tended to have a "loose interpretation" of the Constitution. They believed that the Constitution allowed the federal government to take actions not specifically stated in the document so long as they were necessary for carrying out the government's constitutional responsibilities. (James Madison later opposed the political party known as the Federalists because he did not agree with some of their "loose interpretations." He came to believe that some of their policies violated civil liberties guaranteed by the Constitution.)

Anti-federalists had a different view. Thomas Jefferson, who authored the Declaration of Independence, was an Anti-federalist. Anti-federalists were more suspicious of the Constitution and feared that it gave too much power to the central government. They held to a "strict interpretation." They believed the federal government could only do what the Constitution specifically said. Anti-federalists did not want a small faction of leaders becoming too powerful and using the national government to trample on the rights of citizens. (Thomas Jefferson and James Madison eventually joined forces to lead the Democratic-Republican Party in opposition to the Federalist Party.)

Thomas Jefferson

To make their case for the Constitution, Hamilton and Madison helped author a series of essays known as the *Federalist Papers*. The essays were written to persuade New York's legislature to ratify the Constitution. Eventually, with the support of men like George Washington, Alexander Hamilton, and John Adams, the Federalist view won. Anti-federalists did succeed, however, in securing the Bill of Rights.

THE BILL OF RIGHTS

Congress passed twelve amendments in 1789 for the purpose of protecting civil liberties. The states chose to ratify ten of them. These ten amendments became known as the **Bill of Rights**.

The United States Constitution

First Amendment

The First Amendment guarantees freedom of speech, freedom of the press, freedom to petition the government, and freedom to assemble. It also protects freedom of religion and establishes the principle of separation of church and state. The amendment states that Congress cannot make any law prohibiting the

Freedom of Speech

Freedom of Religion

free exercise of one's religious beliefs. It also forbids Congress from establishing a religion.

Second Amendment

The Second Amendment guarantees the right to bear arms. Although there is much debate today about the private ownership of firearms, in the early days of the nation this right was important because it allowed local communities to maintain militias. Militias are part-time military units made up of private citizens rather than professional soldiers. During colonial times, militias commonly formed to protect small towns. The first shots of the American Revolution were actually fired because British troops attempted to seize arms stored by private citizens at Concord, Massachusetts.

Third Amendment

The Third Amendment restricts quartering (housing) of federal troops in the homes of US citizens. Prior to the revolution, the British angered colonists by forcing them to house British soldiers.

Fourth Amendment

The Fourth Amendment protects citizens against unreasonable searches and seizures. Thanks to this amendment, government officials cannot enter a person's home or go through someone's private property whenever they want. They must have a warrant (official document from a judge) or probable cause (reasonable evidence) that one has committed a crime before they can conduct a search or seize evidence.

Search and Seizure

Fifth Amendment

The Fifth Amendment guarantees **due process**. It sets the rules by which the government may arrest and charge a citizen with a crime. It ensures that no person shall be imprisoned or deprived of their property unjustly. This amendment protects citizens from *double jeopardy* and *self-incrimination*. In other words, a person cannot be tried for the same crime more than once nor can they be forced to testify against themselves in court. Finally, this amendment also places limits on *eminent domain*. Eminent domain is the government's power to take

Due Process

private property for public use. Under the Constitution, the government cannot take a citizen's property without paying "just compensation." For example, if the government takes someone's house, it must pay the owner what the house is worth.

Sixth Amendment

The Sixth Amendment protects the rights of people accused of a crime. This includes the right to a public and speedy trial by jury. A trial by jury means that a group of an accused person's peers decides his or her guilt or innocence, rather than a single government official. This amendment also guarantees the right to legal representation (a lawyer) and the right to call and confront witnesses.

Seventh Amendment

The Seventh Amendment extends the right to a trial by jury to civil cases. Civil cases involve disputes between citizens rather than criminal offenses. For instance, when one party sues another, it is a civil case.

Eighth Amendment

The Eighth Amendment protects those arrested or found guilty of a crime. It prohibits the government from imposing excessive bail and fines. Bail is money an arrested person must pay

Jury Trial

to get out of jail until the date of their trial. Fines are amounts of money a person must pay as punishment for a crime they have been found guilty of. The Eighth Amendment also forbids cruel and unusual punishment of those convicted of a crime. The question of what constitutes "cruel and unusual punishment" is often an issue of debate.

Ninth Amendment

The Ninth Amendment states that the rights specifically mentioned in the Bill of Rights are not the only ones enjoyed by the people.

Tenth Amendment

The Tenth Amendment says that those powers not restricted by the Constitution, nor delegated to the US government, are reserved for the states. In other words, the Constitution grants the states the authority to decide certain matters of law. As mentioned earlier, the Tenth Amendment helps establish federalism.

Louisiana State Capitol Building

Practice 4.1: Foundations of US Politics

1. The major difference between the Articles of Confederation and the United States Constitution was that
   A. the Articles of Confederation governed the colonies before independence, while the Constitution was adopted after independence.
   B. the Constitution was eventually ratified by the states, but the Articles of Confederation never was.
   C. the Articles of Confederation gave most of the power to the states, but the Constitution placed more power in the hands of the federal government.
   D. the Articles of Confederation required a loose interpretation, while the Constitution required a strict interpretation.

2. The Great Compromise settled the issue of
   A. whether or not to keep the Articles of Confederation.
   B. slavery.
   C. how much power states should have.
   D. the structure of the federal legislative branch.

3. How did Federalists and Anti-federalists differ over the Constitution?

4. What is the Bill of Rights, and what purpose does it serve?

4.2 HISTORICAL INFLUENCES ON US GOVERNMENT

ANCIENT MODELS OF GOVERNMENT

Long before the American Revolution, earlier governments laid a foundation for the United States' political system. The ancient **Greeks** practiced direct democracy, allowing each eligible citizen to have a vote. Later, the ancient **Romans** introduced the idea of a republic. Unlike a direct democracy, in which all qualified citizens vote on laws and public policies, in a republic, elected representatives select key leaders and vote on the people's behalf. The framers of the US Constitution ultimately combined elements of both when structuring the United States government.

Roman Senate

BRITISH INFLUENCES

In 1215 AD, a group of English nobles forced King John I to sign the **Magna Carta** or "Great Charter." The document introduced **limited government** to England. Limited government simply means that the government has to obey a set of laws; it is *limited* in what it can do. The Magna Carta granted nobles (upper-class Englishmen) various rights and prevented the king from imposing taxes without the consent of a council. This council eventually became **Parliament**. Parliament established an example of representative democracy that greatly influenced the British colonies. When the United States drafted its Constitution, it included a similar legislative body: Congress.

Signing the Magna Carta

In 1689, the **English Bill of Rights** gave Parliament more power. Under the English Bill of Rights, the monarch could not interfere with Parliamentary elections, nor could he, or she, impose taxes without Parliament's consent. It also granted citizens the right to a speedy trial, outlawed cruel and unusual punishment, and granted citizens the right to petition the government. The US Constitution later guaranteed many of these same rights.

THE MAYFLOWER COMPACT

Signing the Mayflower Compact

In New England, the **Mayflower Compact** set up guidelines for self government. The Puritan settlers at Plymouth, Massachusetts, drafted this document in 1620 while still on board the Mayflower (the ship that brought them to Massachusetts from Europe). It established an elected legislature and stated that the government got its power from the people of the colony. It expressed the colonists' desire to be ruled by a local government, rather than England.

The Declaration of Independence

Second Continental Congress

Young Thomas Jefferson

In May 1775, the Second Continental Congress assembled to discuss how to deal with the outbreak of fighting between the colonies and Great Britain. The following year, in June 1776, delegates to the assembly declared independence from England and appointed a committee to write a statement giving the reasons for this separation. One of the committee's members, a young delegate named Thomas Jefferson, drafted the statement. Jefferson was a man greatly influenced by the Enlightenment and the ideas of Englishman, John Locke. The Enlightenment was a time that featured new ideas about government. Locke was one of the most famous people to come out of this period. Locke believed that people were born with certain **natural rights** that no government could take away. These rights include life, liberty, and property. However, for the good of society, citizens agree to give up certain freedoms and empower governments to maintain order. The right to govern comes from the people. If a government fails to respect its citizens' rights or to fulfill its proper role, then that government should be replaced. Many colonial leaders used Locke's views to justify the American Revolution.

On July 4, 1776, the delegates to the Second Continental Congress formally adopted the **Declaration of Independence**. Appealing to the belief that governments get their power from the people, the Declaration of Independence proclaimed that the United States of America was forevermore a free nation. It asserted the principle of **egalitarianism** (the idea that all men are created equal) and proclaimed that men are born with certain **unalienable rights** (natural rights that government cannot take away). Among these rights are "life, liberty, and the pursuit of happiness." The Declaration of Independence claimed that Great Britain failed to fulfill its duty to respect and uphold these rights. It ends with a list of complaints against the king and states the colonies' right to self-government as a free nation. Sadly, while the Declaration proclaimed equality and freedom, the new nation did not extend the same rights to everyone. Women and while males without property could not vote. Native Americans were not considered citizens and the government often took their land by force. African Americans continued to live in slavery for roughly another century.

Principles of Government Embodied in the US Constitution

Key political principles form the foundation of the US Constitution. The table below lists and defines some of the most important.

Popular Sovereignty	The government rules according to the will of the people.
Individual Liberties	All citizens are born with basic rights like the ones mentioned in the Declaration of Independence and protected by the Bill of Rights. It is the duty of government to respect and uphold these rights.
Checks and Balances	No one branch of government is permitted to become too powerful. Each branch has the ability to check and balance the power of the others.
Due Process of Law	Citizens have certain rights that the government must respect even when charging an individual with a crime. There are laws the government must obey when carrying out criminal proceedings.
Separation of Powers	So that no one leader or group becomes too powerful, the powers of government are split between several branches. Under the Constitution, the federal government is split between the legislative, executive, and judicial branches.
Consent of the Governed	The government gets its power from the people, and the people have the power to take it away.

Practice 4.2: Historical Influences on US Government

1. What contribution did the ancient Greeks make to the United States' political system?

   A. democracy
   B. social contract theory
   C. the Magna Carta
   D. enlightenment

2. The Declaration of Independence proclaimed that people are born with

   A. limited government.
   B. popular sovereignty.
   C. a desire for democracy.
   D. natural rights.

3. List and define three principles on which the US political system is based.

4.3 US Politics in Action

Political Parties

Political Convention

Democrat and Republican Party Symbols

Although they are not mentioned in the Constitution, political parties play an important role in the political process. **Political parties** are organizations that promote political beliefs and sponsor candidates (people running for political office). The United States operates on a *two-party system*. This is a system in which only two main parties dominate a nation's politics. In the United States, these two parties are the **Democrats** and **Republicans**. Both hold positions at the federal, state, and local levels of government. Sometimes, **third parties** (parties other than the Republicans and Democrats) and **independents** (people who are not part of a party) can play an important role in US politics. Third parties usually do well when citizens don't feel that either of the two major parties represents their views. Occasionally, third party or independent candidates win state and local offices, and some even win seats in Congress. Historically, however, they have not won the presidency or large numbers of congressional seats. This is largely because of the challenges they face. They have less money and fewer members than the Republican and Democratic parties. Also, because third parties usually rally around a single issue or regional concern, they often have trouble appealing to a national audience.

Party Structure and Function

Political parties serve several functions. They nominate candidates for office, limit the voting choice to candidates who have a real chance of winning (usually the Republican and Democratic candidates), help the different branches of government communicate, and establish **party platforms**. The platform is the party's statement of programs and policies it will pursue once its candidates are in office. It is made up of several *planks*. Each plank is a separate policy. For example, if the Republican platform states that the party opposes abortion, favors increased military spending, and supports a

Current Chairman of the Democratic National Committee Howard Dean

constitutional amendment against flag burning, then each one of these issues represents one plank of the platform. Parties normally adopt their platform every four years at their national convention. The **national convention** is a gathering of party delegates from each state and US territory that meet to nominate candidates for president and vice president in the upcoming general election.

AFFECTING CHANGE IN A DEMOCRATIC SOCIETY

ELECTIONS

The United States is a democracy. Citizens elect the people they want to serve as public officials. Elections are one of the best ways citizens can affect change under the US political system. Citizens vote local, state, and federal officials into office by means of a **general election**. General elections are held in November of an election year. This is the time when voters choose between the Republican, Democratic, and any third party or independent candidates for public office. However, before the general election is held, each party must decide which candidate will be its representative. After all, there may be ten Democrats who want to be president, or six Republicans who want to run for governor. To decide on a single nominee, each major party holds primary elections a few months before the general election. In **primary elections**, voters choose between candidates within the same party. The candidate who wins the primaries receives the party's

Caucus

nomination. Some states, such as Iowa, choose their party's nominee for president by means of a **caucus**. In a caucus, party members hold local meetings to choose delegates who vote in favor of nominating a certain candidate at the national convention.

POLITICAL ACTIVISM

Political activism enables private citizens to make their opinions known and their voices heard. Voting is one way people are politically active. Another way citizens exercise influence is through a **petition**. Petitions often take the form of a document signed by a large number of citizens. They empower citizens to force political leaders to vote on a certain issue or pass a certain policy. If citizens are extremely displeased with a public official they can ask for a **recall election**. Recall elections are special votes called to determine if voters want to remove a sitting official from office before his or her elected term is up. Citizens who feel that current laws are unjust might practice **civil disobedience**. Civil disobedience occurs when citizens peacefully and non-violently refuse to obey a certain law. For example, during the 1960s, many establishments were segregated (forced blacks and whites to sit in separate areas). African Americans thought this was unfair because whites usually enjoyed better facilities. As a result, civil rights protestors often practiced civil disobedience. They peacefully sat in all-white areas until they were arrested or served. These protests were called "sit-ins," and they eventually helped end segregation.

Other forms of political protests include:

- **Marches** – Political marches involve people marching together in support of a political cause. Usually they involve marching to some symbolic location, like a state capital or national monument.
- **Rallies** – Political rallies are group gatherings held in support of a cause. They usually involve speeches that call on people to take some kind of political action.
- **Boycotts** – A boycott is when a group of citizens decides not to do business with a company or government body in hopes of forcing it to change some policy. For instance, when buses in Montgomery, Alabama, required whites and blacks to sit separately, African Americans launched a bus boycott during the 1950s. They refused to ride the buses until the law was changed. This cost the city of Montgomery a lot of money and helped lead to the end of segregation on buses.
- **Strikes** – Strikes are when people refuse to work until some policy is changed. Usually, strikes are meant to make an employer change the way they treat their employees. However, sometimes a strike can be aimed at changing government policies as well.

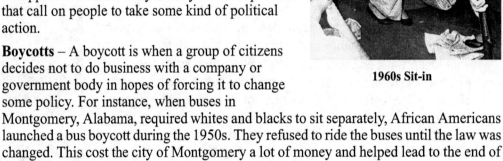

1960s Sit-in

POLITICAL COMPROMISE

As mentioned in section 4.1, a **compromise** is an agreement reached when two parties who disagree with one another each give up a little of what they want to come to a conclusion both sides can live with. Earlier we read how compromises played an important role at the Constitutional Convention. Compromise continues to be an important part of US politics today. Leaders constantly use compromise to pass laws, form policies, and effectively lead at all levels of government.

Political Compromise

AMENDMENTS AND IMPEACHMENT

The framers of the Constitution wanted to make sure that leaders and citizens could correct political mistakes. Therefore, they put several key provisions in the Constitution. One is **impeachment**. As discussed in chapter 3, impeachment is a process by which public officials guilty of wrongdoing can be removed from office. Another provision is the **amendment process**. Amendments are simply changes to the Constitution. In the case of the United States Constitution, they are always added at the end of the document. Currently, there are twenty-seven amendments. The first ten were added as Bill of Rights. The most recent was ratified in 1992. There are two ways that amendments may be added to the Constitution. First, if two-thirds of both houses of Congress vote in favor of a change, the proposed amendment is presented to the states. If three-fourths of the states approve the proposed amendment, it becomes part of the Constitution. The second way that an amendment can be added is when two-thirds of the states call for a constitutional convention. Any amendments adopted by the convention must then be ratified by three-fourths of the states.

CITIZEN RIGHTS AND RESPONSIBILITIES

President and First Lady Nixon Leave Washington After the President Resigns to Avoid Impeachment

Under the Constitution, US citizens have certain rights (review section 4.1 regarding the Bill of Rights). However, in order for the US political system to function, they also have to be willing to accept responsibilities. Below is a table listing some of these key responsibilities:

Military Service	Although there have been times in US history where the government drafted (required) people to serve in the military, currently, the US military is a volunteer force. Citizens must be willing to volunteer to serve in the military in order for the United States to maintain a defense and protect its national security.
Jury Duty	The Sixth Amendment guarantees the right to a trial by jury. The Seventh Amendment extends this right to civil cases. The purpose of a jury is to make sure that private citizens, not the government, decide the guilt or innocence of someone accused of a crime. However, in order for this system to work, citizens must be willing to sacrifice time, energy, and sometimes money to serve on juries.
Paying Taxes	A tax is money paid to the government. Nobody likes paying taxes. However, without tax revenue, the government could not carry out its duties under the Constitution. Therefore, to enjoy the freedoms offered under our US political system, citizens must be willing to pay the taxes required by law.
Obeying Laws	Since society cannot function without law and order, citizens must obey the laws of their city, county, state, and nation.
Serving in Public Office	The United States political system relies on citizens who are willing to serve in public office. If citizens were not willing to serve, there would be no one to vote for and democracy would not work. For this reason, citizens should consider serving in public office. Those who don't serve should still educate themselves about issues and actively support candidates they feel would best serve the interests of the people.

Qualifications and Requirements for US Citizenship

In order to be a citizen of the United States of America, one must meet certain qualifications. Under current US law, the following individuals qualify as US citizens:

Natural born citizens	Anyone born in the United States
Born to US Citizens Abroad	If someone is born outside the United States to two parents who are US citizens, then that person is usually considered a US citizen as well. If someone is born outside the United States to parents, only one of which is a US citizen, then the person is considered a citizen provided that the citizen parent lived in the US at least five years prior to the birth and at least two of those five years were after the parent's fourteenth birthday.
Naturalization	Naturalization is a process by which foreign-born people may become US citizens. Naturalized citizens must: 1. be at least 18 years of age. 2. be a legal permanent resident. 3. have been physically present in the country for a specified amount of time. (The required amount of time varies from case to case based on certain individual factors.) 4. be a person of "good moral character." 5. pass a citizenship test on US government and history. 6. have a basic knowledge of the English language. 7. take an oath of allegiance to the United States.

Practice 4.3: US Politics in Action

1. Political parties are

   A. conventions where delegates nominate people to run for office.

   B. statements of programs a group of political candidates stand for.

   C. organizations that promote political beliefs and sponsor candidates.

   D. groups that primarily devote their time and energy to organizing acts of civil disobedience.

2. The US political system operates on a

   A. multi-party system.   C. third-party system.

   B. two-party system.   D. independent system.

3. Brian and Claudine both feel that a government policy regarding lunch counters in federal buildings discriminates against short people. They join a group of fellow vertically-challenged citizens and peacefully sit at a counter normally reserved for basketball players. They demand to be served or arrested. Brian and Claudine have just participated in

   A. a protest rally.   C. a boycott.

   B. one plank of a political platform.   D. an act of civil disobedience.

4. Describe two ways amendments can be added to the Constitution.

5. List three responsibilities US citizens should be prepared to fulfill.

4.4 THE UNITED STATES AND OTHER NATIONS

Many different countries make up the world we live in. These nations are often divided into states and provinces. The United States must exist as part of this larger worldwide community. In order to provide peace and prosperity, the Constitution puts in place a political system that helps the US effectively communicate with other countries.

DIPLOMACY AND AID

English Prime Minister Gordon Brown, left, and President Barack Obama

A number of issues require US **diplomacy**. Diplomacy occurs when world leaders meet to discuss and work out peaceful solutions to international problems. Trade policies, economic concerns, territory disputes, and human rights issues are all commonly addressed through diplomacy. Effective diplomacy often results in **treaties**. Treaties are formal agreements between nations. Leaders sign treaties to promise a certain action will be taken by their country in return for promised action from another country. In the past, treaties have been signed pledging to respect international trade routes, prevent the spread of nuclear weapons, help another nation defend itself against attack, and so on. Under the Constitution, the president of the United States has the authority to negotiate and sign treaties. However, as we learned when we read about checks and balances, the United States Senate must ratify any treaty before it becomes official.

Economic and Humanitarian Aid

Economic and humanitarian aid can be another positive result of diplomacy. Many times, economically developed countries like the US will give money, manpower, and needed technology to less developed nations. Sometimes, this relief comes as a response to some natural disaster, like a famine, earthquake, or tsunami. At other times, nations receive aid simply because their economy is struggling and needs help. When possible, the United States has often supplied aid to countries in hopes of establishing good relations and preventing the rise of governments that might not support US interests.

TRADE

Trade is the exchange of goods between countries. *Exports* are goods a nation sells to other countries. Exports bring money into a country and help the economy. *Imports* are goods a nation buys from other countries. Money spent on imported products goes out of the country and into the economy of the nations that produced the goods. **Free trade** exists when there are no barriers or limitations on trade. Producers are free to sell their goods in other countries. Consumer demand alone decides which goods are bought and how much they cost.

Free Trade in the US

However, countries often do not allow free trade. Sometimes, in order to protect their own producers, countries will impose **tariffs**. Tariffs are taxes on imports. They raise the price of foreign goods and make domestic goods (goods produced in the country) more competitive in the market place.

Sometimes, trade can be used to pressure countries to take certain actions or to change existing policies. **Sanctions** are limitations on trade with a certain country. Nations often agree to impose sanctions in order to force a country to change its behavior. For example, during the 1970s and '80s, a number of nations limited trade with South Africa because of its racist political system known as *apartheid*. Many

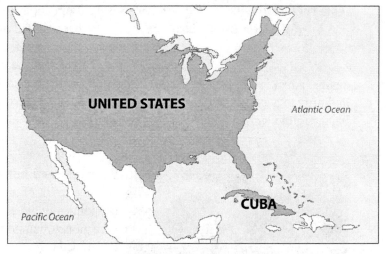
The United States and Cuba

of these sanctions remained in place until South Africa finally ended apartheid in the early '90s. Even more drastic are **embargoes**. An embargo means that trade with a particular country is cut off entirely. Once again, embargoes are meant to influence the behavior of a foreign country. For over forty years, the United States has imposed an embargo against the communist state of Cuba. Although Cuba is just ninety miles from Florida, no Cuban goods may be legally imported into the US, and no US goods may be legally exported to Cuba.

Chapter 4

CARRYING OUT US FOREIGN POLICY

President James Monroe

The executive branch forms and carries out US foreign policy. **Foreign policy** refers to how the US government chooses to conduct its relations with other countries. One of the earliest examples of how the executive branch sets foreign policy was the **Monroe Doctrine**. The policy was called the *Monroe Doctrine* because President James Monroe established it in 1823. The doctrine stated that the United States would not accept Europe interfering in the Western Hemisphere and that the Americas were no longer open to colonization. The Monroe Doctrine helped reinforce the presidency's key role in deciding the direction of US foreign policy.

Ann Wagner, Ambassador to Luxembourg **Antonio O. Garza Jr., Ambassador to Mexico**
US Ambassadors

There are several ways the executive branch carries out foreign policy. One of the most common is through **US ambassadors**. An ambassador is a public official who represents their government in a foreign country. The United States has ambassadors in most countries around the world. The ambassador will often meet and communicate with leaders of other countries on the president's behalf. Sometimes, when major issues are at stake, the president will rely on his or her **secretary of state**. The secretary of state is part of the president's cabinet and is responsible for relations with other nations. Often, the secretary of state will visit other countries to meet with foreign leaders, or will host ambassadors of other nations in efforts to carry out foreign policy. Sometimes, the president will call foreign leaders directly or meet with them personally as part of a **presidential summit**. A summit is a meeting of world leaders. It can involve the leaders of only two countries, or several leaders from around the world. In recent decades, US presidents have participated in summits to discuss economic sanctions, nuclear weapons, environmental issues, terrorism, and many other important matters. Summits often result in better foreign relations and sometimes in formal treaties

Former Secretary of State Condoleeza Rice Meeting with Foreign Leaders

Presidential Summit Meeting

The most drastic foreign policy action a president can take is **military action**. Sometimes military action might only involve a single act, such as when President Bill Clinton ordered a missile strike against terrorist training camps in Afghanistan in 1998. Other times, it can involve an ongoing war, such as President George W. Bush's decision to invade Afghanistan and Iraq as part of the "war on terror." Because military action often involves the loss of human life and destruction of property, it is usually reserved as a last resort.

COMMON FOREIGN POLICY ISSUES

A number of issues commonly affect US foreign policy. One is **isolationism**. Isolationists believe that the US should focus mainly on matters at home. They don't believe the US should become involved in international disputes nor commit the US military to settling foreign conflicts. Prior to World War II, isolationism was a popular sentiment in the United States. After the war, however, the US government became concerned about the spread of communism. Many citizens became convinced that the Soviet Union would stop at nothing short of world domination. Isolationism began to fade. Although fears about communism have subsided since the end of the Cold War, today's world is so connected by technology, communications, business, and international relationships, that few political leaders believe true isolationism will ever be possible again.

Military Action

Economic interests and national security are also important issues. **Economic interests** include business connections, trade agreements, foreign investments, and access to needed foreign goods and resources that keep the US economy growing and strong. Failure to protect international economic interests can damage the US economy, lead to failed businesses, higher unemployment, and financial problems for millions of Americans. **National security** involves protecting the country from outside threats, such as a military attack or terrorism. The executive branch is responsible for having a foreign policy that protects both national security and economic interests.

Chapter 4

THE UNITED NATIONS

UN Building

Pope Benedict XVI Waits to Address the
UN General Assembly

The **United Nations** is an international organization devoted to helping nations engage in diplomacy and find peaceful solutions to problems. World leaders founded the UN after World War II. It is located in New York City. Ambassadors from member nations meet at the UN, negotiate their differences, and seek to promote peace while working together to deal with international problems and provide needed humanitarian aid.

Practice 4.4: The United States and other Nations

1. When world leaders meet to work out peaceful solutions to problems it is called
   A. diplomacy.   B. sanctions.   C. isolationism.   D. free trade.

2. Treaties, humanitarian aid, diplomacy, negotiations, and sometimes military action are all part of
   A. sanctions.   C. economic aid.
   B. isolationism.   D. foreign policy.

3. Dakota is a high-ranking US official. Although he represents the United States government, he lives in Madrid, Spain, and is authorized to speak for the president on issues regarding US-Spanish relations. Dakota is most likely
   A. the secretary of state.   C. part of a presidential summit.
   B. someone who opposes free trade.   D. a US ambassador.

CHAPTER 4 REVIEW

Key People, Terms, and Concepts

Second Continental Congress
Articles of Confederation
Shays' Rebellion
Compromise
Virginia Plan
New Jersey Plan
Great Compromise
Connecticut Plan
Three-fifths Compromise
Slave Trade compromise
United States Constitution
Bill of Rights
Federalists
anti-federalists
Federalist Papers
Greek influences on US government
Roman influences on US government
Magna Carta
limited government
Parliament
English Bill of Rights
Mayflower Compact
natural rights
Declaration of Independence
egalitarianism
unalienable (inalienable) rights
popular sovereignty
individual liberties
checks and balances
due process of law
separation of powers
consent of the governed
political parties
two-party system

Republicans and Democrats
third parties and independents
party platform
national convention
general election
primary election
caucus
political activism
petition
recall election
civil disobedience
marches, rallies, boycotts, and strikes
impeachment
amendment process
citizen rights and responsibilities
qualifications of citizenship
diplomacy
treaties
economic and humanitarian aid
trade
free trade
tariffs
sanctions
embargoes
foreign policy
Monroe Doctrine
US ambassadors
secretary of state
presidential summit
military action
isolationism
economic interest
national security
United Nations

Chapter 4

Multiple Choice Questions

1. Shays' Rebellion helped convince US leaders that it was time for a/an
    A. citizenship test.
    B. change in the Articles of Confederation.
    C. amendment to the Constitution.
    D. presidential summit.

> "I cannot accept this proposal. Why should we, merely because of our size, be left with less of a voice in the national government? Did our sons not bleed for liberty just as the sons of Virginia and Pennsylvania? No, we shall not surrender our future to the whims of other states."

2. The quote above is most likely opposing
    A. the Articles of Confederation.
    B. the Bill of Rights.
    C. the New Jersey Plan.
    D. the Virginia Plan.

3. Which of the following would be most concerning to a Federalist?
    A. giving too much power to the national government
    B. interpreting the Constitution too loosely
    C. failing to give the president enough power
    D. not doing enough to protect the rights of states

4. Edward's parents were both born in Louisiana, met in New Orleans, and moved to Minnesota where they lived for seven years. Two years ago, they moved to France, where Edward was born three months ago. If Edward wants to become a US citizen, he will need to
    A. move to the United States before he turns fourteen.
    B. take a citizenship test.
    C. live in the United States at least five years.
    D. do nothing, because he is already a US citizen.

5. The body of laws that replaced the Articles of Confederation and still serves as the basis of the US political system today is the
    A. US Constitution.
    B. Bill of Rights.
    C. Federalist Papers.
    D. Qualifications of Citizenship.

6. Serving in office, obeying laws, paying taxes, and volunteering to join the Navy are all ways citizens

    A. exercise their rights.
    B. benefit from due process.
    C. fulfill their responsibilities.
    D. engage in political activism.

7. George is arrested and charged with a crime because he made public statements criticizing Congress. George claims that he cannot be punished because the Constitution guarantees his freedom of speech. What is George appealing to?

    A. his citizenship qualifications
    B. the Bill of Rights
    C. his political party
    D. the Federalists Papers

8. The president desperately wants to settle a trade dispute with China as peacefully as possible. He hopes to obtain a compromise that will benefit both countries. The president will most likely start by using

    A. sanctions.
    B. embargoes.
    C. diplomacy.
    D. military action.

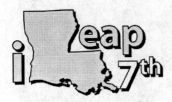

Chapter 5
Historical Thinking Skills

This chapter addresses the following Louisiana iLeap standards:

H-1A-MI:	43. Construct a timeline of key events and key figures in U.S. history from 1763 to 1877
	44. Interpret a timeline to identify cause-and-effect relationships among events in U.S. history
H-1A-M2:	45. Explain the point of view of key historical figures and groups in U.S. history
H-1A-M3:	46. Explain the causes, effects, or impact of a given historical event in U.S. history
	47. Explain how a given historical figure influenced or changed the course of U.S. history
H-1A-M4:	48. Compare and contrast two primary sources related to the same event in U.S. history
H-1A-M5:	49. Propose and defend an alternative course of action to a given issue or problem in U.S. history
H-1A-M6:	50. Conduct historical research using a variety of resources, and evaluate those resources for reliability and bias, to answer historical questions related to U.S. history

5.1 CHRONOLOGICAL RELATIONSHIPS AND PATTERNS

There are different ways one can study history. One is the use of **timelines**. A timeline is a line that shows when key events occurred and major figures lived in US history. Below is an example of a timeline of events for World War II.

World War II

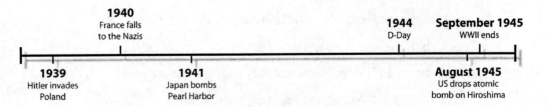

Historical Thinking Skills

Practice 5.1: Chronological Relationships and Patterns

Look at the list of historical events below to complete exercise 5.1 and answer questions 2–4.

The Progressive Era　　　　　　　　**The War in Iraq**

- Progressive Era – late 1800s – early 1900s.
- Great Depression – 1930s
- US enters World War II – 1941
- John F. Kennedy elected president of the United States – 1960
- Persian Gulf War – 1991
- Iraq War begins – 2003

1. Construct a timeline depicting the above events in US history chronologically (in order of when they happened).

2. Where on the timeline would you place President Kennedy's assassination?
   A. between the Progressive Era and World War II
   B. between the Persian Gulf and Iraq wars
   C. between Kennedy being elected president and the Persian Gulf War
   D. between World War II and Kennedy being elected president.

3. Where on the timeline would you place Japan's surrender in World War II?
   A. between the Great Depression and the US entering World War II
   B. between the Progressive Era and the Great Depression
   C. between the Progressive Era and World War II
   D. between the US entering World War II and Kennedy's election

4. Where on the timeline would you place the election of President George W. Bush in 2000?
   A. between Kennedy's election and the Persian Gulf War
   B. between the Persian Gulf War and the Iraq War
   C. between World War II and Kennedy's election
   D. between the Progressive Era and the Persian Gulf War

5.2 IMPACT OF PEOPLE AND EVENTS ON HISTORY

HISTORICAL POINTS OF VIEW

When studying history, it is important to consider **different historical points of view**. Not everyone involved in a historic event viewed things the same way. Take for instance, the American Revolution. Many colonists saw the revolution as a brave struggle for independence. Rich merchants, large landowners, and middle-class citizens benefited greatly from breaking ties with Great Britain. Small farmers and poor whites along the frontier, however, often had no interest in the revolution or

American Revolution

in remaining loyal to England. Following independence, they still struggled economically. Meanwhile, the new nation did not recognize Native Americans as citizens and continued to keep African Americans enslaved. Women were not treated equal to men and had no right to vote. How do you think poor whites, Native Americans, African Americans, and women may have viewed the effects of the American Revolution differently from wealthy white males and middle-class citizens?

Studying different points of view is also important when studying US expansion. During the 1800s, the United States claimed new territories west of the Mississippi River. From the viewpoint of the US government and many white settlers, those that ventured west were heroic figures fulfilling the nation's destiny. But what about the Native Americans who were forced off of their land? Many of them suffered greatly as the US government forced them to move and often failed to keep its promises. Studying different points of view serves to broaden one's understanding of US history.

By trying to understand how different people viewed the same event, you can gain a better understanding of why people responded the way they did and what lessons can be learned for the future. When historians and students fail to consider different points of view, they run the risk of settling for a limited or inaccurate understanding of history.

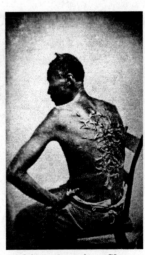
African American Slave

Historical Thinking Skills

States' Rights Debate

RECOGNIZING CAUSES AND EFFECTS IN US HISTORY

Historians (people who study history for a living) spend much of their time studying **causes and effects**. They try to determine what factors caused certain events in history and what effects these events had on things that

Segregation

The Civil Rights Movement

happened later. For example, despite opposition from some states, the delegates to the Constitutional Convention elected to allow slavery under the Constitution. They did this because much of the nation's economy depended on slave labor. As more countries outlawed slavery and the US economy changed, the North and South became divided. This led to the Civil War and the deaths of more than 600,000 Americans. Even after the war, racism remained. For over 100 years, laws segregating African Americans from whites remained in place and led to continued oppression. Eventually, such oppression led to a civil rights movement. The civil rights movement led to laws and decisions by the Supreme Court that greatly broadened the powers of the federal government and lessened the powers of the states. Even today, the African American community faces challenges many trace back to the impact of slavery. These issues still remain important in US politics in the twenty-first century.

Chapter 5

Constitutional Convention

Event:	delegates to the Constitutional Convention's allow slavery
Cause:	much of the United States relied on slavery economically
Effects:	divisions between the North and South
	Civil War
	unjust segregation laws
	civil rights movement
	broader powers for federal government; less power for states
	modern-day concerns for the African American community

This is one example of historical causes and effects that historians study in an effort to better understand the past so that society can learn important lessons for the future.

Practice 5.2: Impact of People and Events on History

1. Why do you think it is important to study historical events from the viewpoint of more than one person or group?

2. In chapters 1–4, we read about several historical events as we examined geography's impact on US history and basic principles of the United States government. Use some of the events we've covered to show the causes and effects of historical events.

5.3 Historical Research

Researching Historical Questions

United States National Archives

Historians rely on **research** to find answers to historical questions. Research takes many forms. Often, historians rely on **archives**. Archives are collections of historical records. Governments, companies, institutions, churches, and so on, all commonly maintain archives. Archives are very valuable to historical research because they contain **primary sources**. Primary sources provide historians with original writings, documents, videos, and more that contain historical information. Letters, newspapers, government memos, diaries, and interviews with people directly involved in the historical events are all examples of primary sources. Primary sources exist in places other than archives, but archives are important because they usually provide historians with many primary sources in one place.

Historians Conducting Research

Historian Edmund Morgan at Yale University

Historians also rely on **secondary sources**. Secondary sources include any works done by previous historians that one can use in his or her own research. For instance, let's say you have to do a report on President John F. Kennedy for class. As part of your research, you read a biography about President Kennedy's life. Next, you study two or three encyclopedia articles. Finally, you watch a respected documentary about his presidency on public television. The biography, the encyclopedia entries, and the documentary are all secondary sources. Someone else did the primary research, but you are using their findings to help you in your own research. If, on the other hand, you were lucky enough to get your hands on White House memos, personal diaries from people who worked for Kennedy, and tape recordings of conversations between officials who were actually involved in the Kennedy presidency, these would be primary sources. Secondary sources are valuable and helpful when conducting research. However, serious historians do their best to obtain as many primary sources as they can. Primary sources allow them to study people and events without being influenced by the opinions of other historians.

Through research, historians gather **historical data** (facts about the past). The task of the historian is to analyze this data to determine cause and effects of historical events and to determine how different people and groups may have viewed the issues and events of their day.

EVALUATING ALTERNATIVES

Historians' research often leads them to believe that there were **alternative courses of action** in history. In other words, they come to the conclusion that events could have happened differently or had a different effect than they historically did. For example, what if the Founding Fathers had not made certain compromises at the Constitutional Convention? How would that have changed US history? What if a particular president had made a different decision about this, or that, economic, political, or military issue? What if Lincoln had lived to oversee southern reconstruction, rather than being assassinated? What if the US government had not insisted on taking land occupied by Native Americans during the nineteenth century? Historians don't study the past simply to learn the facts. They want to know if the decisions that were made were the right ones. They try to determine *why* things happened the way they did and find possible alternatives. By understanding alternative decisions that could have been made in the past, historians hope to offer valuable information that can help governments and citizens make wiser decisions in the future.

Student Discussion

Practice 5.3: Historical Research

1. Encyclopedia's and US history text books are examples of

    A. alternative courses.

    B. primary sources.

    C. secondary sources.

    D. archives.

2. Phil conducts research on the War of 1812. After studying secondary and primary sources, Phil writes a paper arguing that the region of New England would be better off today if it had seceded from the Union during the war. It appears Phil is

    A. ignoring historical data.

    B. suggesting an alternative course of action.

    C. rejecting archive research.

    D. using too many primary sources.

3. List three or four ways historians and students can conduct research.

CHAPTER 5 REVIEW

Key Terms, People, and Concepts

timelines	archives
different historical points of view	primary sources
historians	secondary sources
historical causes and effects	historical data
historical research	alternative courses of action

Read chapters 6–9, then come back to this page and do the following exercises individually or in groups.

1. Construct a timeline that records 10 to 20 key events in US history from 1763 to 1877.

2. Explain how your timeline demonstrates causes and effects in US history.

3. Pick two key issues or events in US history. Present a written page for each describing how you think each event or issue was viewed by different groups or individuals who lived during the period.

4. Pick a historical figure and explain how he, or she, influenced or changed US history.

5. Choose a topic in US history and make a list of primary and secondary resources that would be useful in researching your topic. Conduct research on your topic using at least three different resources and write a report. Consult with your teacher for help choosing a topic and deciding on research resources.

Chapter 6
US History: Birth of a Nation

This chapter addresses the following Louisiana iLeap standards:

H-IB-M6	51. Explain the causes, course, and consequences of the American Revolutionary War
	52. Compare and contrast the strategies and motivations of the Patriots, Loyalists, and British during the American Revolution
	53. Explain the role of key figures in the American Revolution
H-IB-M7	54. Explain how the American Revolution affected the politics, society, and economy of the new nation
H-IB-M8	55. Describe the issues involved in the creation and ratification of the U.S. Constitution
	56. Explain the significance of the Bill of Rights and its specific guarantees
	57. Describe major events and issues involving early presidencies

6.1 THE AMERICAN REVOLUTION

CAUSES OF THE REVOLUTION

From 1754 to 1763, Great Britain battled France for control of North America. After a long war that involved fighting around the world, France finally surrendered. Soon after, King George III issued the **Proclamation of 1763**. This order prevented colonists from moving west of the Appalachian Mountains. Among other things, the king hoped to improve relations with Native Americans and strengthen control over the area. Colonists, however, resented the order. They wanted the rich land and resources the region offered. Many of them ignored the king's proclamation.

King George III

US History: Birth of a Nation

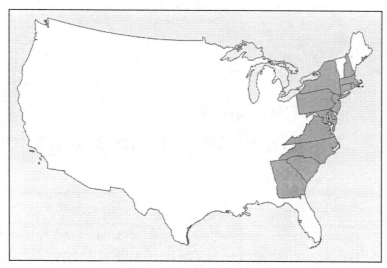

The Thirteen Colonies in 1776

Following its victory over France, Britain had a huge war debt. Since the war had been fought largely to protect the British colonists, the king and Parliament reasoned that the colonies should help cover the cost. As a result, Parliament passed a series of laws meant to ensure that the American colonists paid their fair share. One of the laws that made colonists the angriest was the **Stamp Act** in 1765. Although it was not the first tax passed, it was one of the most offensive because it affected nearly everyone trying to conduct business. The Stamp Act created a tax on all legal documents, licenses, newspapers, and so on. It required that all documents have a government stamp. Before you could get the stamp, you had to pay the tax. Many colonists were angry and protested: "No taxation without representation!" Since the colonists had no one representing them in Parliament when it passed new taxes, they believed they should not have to pay them. Soon, protests against the Stamp Act spread throughout the colonies. Many colonists became **patriots**. Patriots opposed Great Britain's policies and eventually called for independence. Others colonists remained **loyalists**. (Patriots called them "tories.") Loyalists were colonists who remained loyal to the king and wanted to remain part of Great Britain.

THE SONS OF LIBERTY

The Sons of Liberty Intimidate a Loyalist

A number of patriots called for boycotts. Colonial boycotts were protests in which people refused to buy British products. Organizers of boycotts hoped that British businesses would get tired of losing money and pressure Parliament to change the law. Patriot groups like the **Sons of Liberty** formed in several colonies. The Sons of Liberty protested laws like the Stamp Act. They used violence and threats to make sure no one sold stamps and that everyone stuck to the boycotts.

Chapter 6

CONFLICT IN BOSTON

In 1767, Parliament passed the **Townshend Acts**. These laws taxed imported goods like glass and tea. So violent was colonial reaction to the Townshend Acts that England sent troops to Boston. On March 5, 1770, British soldiers who felt threatened by a mob of angry protesters fired shots that left several colonists dead or dying. The event became known as the **Boston Massacre.**

The Boston Massacre

Shortly after the "massacre," Parliament repealed the Townshend Acts and tensions lessened. They did not, however, go away. More and more Americans would not accept England's control over them. Several colonies organized **Committees of Correspondence**. These were patriot groups dedicated to organizing colonial resistance against the Crown. One law that angered the Committees of Correspondence was the **Tea Act**. Under the Tea Act, Britain's East India Company was allowed to sell tea in the colonies without paying the normal tax. This allowed the company to sell tea for less money. At first, Britain thought it would win favor with the colonies for selling the tea at a cheaper price. Many patriots, however, saw this as a trick to get the colonies to stop boycotting British goods. They called for boycotts against British tea and continued to criticize British rule. In December 1773, members of Boston's Committee of Correspondence called for drastic action to protest the law. Boston patriots dressed as Mohawk Indians and marched to Boston Harbor. There, in what became known as the **Boston Tea Party**, they raided ships hauling British tea and threw the crates overboard. In response, Parliament passed the **Intolerable Acts**. These acts closed Boston Harbor and placed a military governor over Massachusetts. England also expanded the Canadian border, taking land away from certain colonies.

The Boston Tea Party

British Troops in Boston

The "Shot Heard 'Round the World"

Thomas Paine

Although patriots called for independence, many colonists still hoped for a peaceful solution. In April 1775, however, all hope of a peaceful resolution was lost. As British troops made their way to seize arms and ammunition at Concord, Massachusetts, tcolonial militia met them at Lexington. It was there that someone (to this day no one is sure who) fired the "shot heard 'round the world" that started the American Revolution. In January 1776, a patriot writer named **Thomas Paine** published his famous pamphlet, ***Common Sense***. In it, he made a strong case for independence that won many to the cause. Later that same year, Thomas Jefferson wrote the **Declaration of Independence**. Resistance to British laws had grown into a full-blown revolution.

Key Figures of the American Revolution

A number of key people played major roles in the American Revolution. Below is a list of some of the most important figures and the contributions they made to the struggle for independence.

George Washington

George Washington was a Virginia landowner who had fought for the British during the French and Indian War. The Continental Congress chose Washington to lead the new nation's Continental Army during the Revolution. Against all odds, Washington overcame early defeats and a lack of troops and supplies to lead the Continental Army to victory. Unlike many generals in world history, he chose to surrender his command after the revolution, rather than using his position to seize personal power. He later presided over the Constitutional Convention and was elected by the first Electoral College to serve as the United States' first president.

Chapter 6

Benjamin Franklin

Benjamin Franklin was a respected inventor, scientist, and writer, who served as the colonies' ambassador to Great Britain prior to the revolution. At first, he hoped to maintain peace and unity between the colonies and Britain. However, he eventually became convinced that independence was the only solution and supported the revolutionary cause. During the revolution, Franklin put his diplomatic skills to work. He represented the new nation in France, where he eventually secured key help from the French military that helped the United States win independence.

Samuel Adams

Samuel Adams was a fiery patriot and one of the first voices calling for independence. A brewer and mediocre businessman, Adams's gift was his public speaking. With his passionate speeches, he won many to the patriot cause. A Bostonian, he became one of Massachusetts's representatives to the Continental Congress and supported the Declaration of Independence. He helped draft both the Articles of Confederation and Massachusetts's first state constitution.

John Adams

The second cousin of Samuel Adams, John Adams was a Bostonian lawyer who supported independence. He gained a reputation as a strong patriot, opposing the Stamp Act. He represented Massachusetts in the First and Second Continental Congress, and he was the one to nominate George Washington to be commander of the colonial army. He was among those selected to help Thomas Jefferson draft the Declaration of Independence. For much of the war, he served as an ambassador to Europe. He later became the United States' first vice president and its second president.

Thomas Jefferson

Virginian Thomas Jefferson was a young delegate to the Second Continental Congress when he drafted most of the Declaration of Independence in 1776. During the war he served for two years as the governor of Virginia. After the revolution he served as the United States' ambassador to France. He eventually won election as the third president of the United States in 1800.

John Hancock

A wealthy Bostonian merchant, John Hancock was one of the first major leaders of the movement for independence in New England. He served as president of the Continental Congress and was the first person to sign the Declaration of Independence. He later served as president of the Congress of the Confederation (the legislative body that governed the nation under the Articles of Confederation) and as the first governor of Massachusetts. Hancock was enraged when his good friend, John Adams, nominated George Washington to lead the American army because Hancock, himself, wanted the job.

Patrick Henry

Patrick Henry was a radical supporter of independence. He is most famous for a speech he gave before the Virginia legislature on March 23, 1775. Henry convinced Virginia to commit troops to the cause of independence with his fiery words: "…give me liberty, or give me death!" Although some historians debate whether or not Henry actually said these exact words, he definitely helped convince Virginia to commit to the revolution.

George Rogers Clark

At less than thirty years of age, George Rogers Clark won fame as the commander of Continental Army forces in the western territories of Kentucky and beyond the Ohio River. Because Great Britain agreed to surrender this territory as part of the treaty ending the war, some have hailed Clark as the "Conqueror of the Northwest." Clark's younger brother, William Clark, later helped lead the historical Lewis and Clark Expedition.

THE FIRST YEAR OF THE REVOLUTION

The American Revolution began long before the Continental Congress signed the Declaration of Independence. By the summer of 1776, colonists and British forces had been fighting for over a year. King George III of England did not expect a long war. After all, the British had one of the world's most powerful armies and its mightiest navy. How could a bunch of untrained colonists possibly defeat them? The colonists, however, were fighting for their homeland and the right to govern themselves. They were more determined to win the war. Colonial leaders also knew they would all hang for treason if the revolution failed. The American colonists had no choice but victory!

Fort Ticonderoga

TICONDEROGA AND BOSTON

Ethan Allen and the Green Mountain Boys

In May 1775, a patriot force from Vermont known as the Green Mountain Boys launched a surprise raid on a small British force stationed at **Fort Ticonderoga**. Making their way through an opening in the wall, the Green Mountain Boys took the fort without firing a single shot. The victory at Ticonderoga was small, but it provided the patriots with desperately needed cannons and ammunition.

After Lexington and Concord, nearly 20,000 patriots surrounded the British in Boston. In June 1775, British troops launched a series of attacks against two hills occupied by American forces. The British eventually won the battle but many of their men were killed or wounded. Although most of the bloodiest fighting took place on Breed's Hill, the battle was named for the second hill and became known as the Battle of Bunker Hill. A month later, General George Washington arrived. His forces seized key high ground and, with the help of cannons hauled from Fort Ticonderoga, gained an advantage over the British.

NEW YORK AND NEW JERSEY

Washington Crossing the Delaware River

In March, 1776, the British left Boston by ship and made their way to New York. Washington moved south to meet them. Once they arrived, the stronger British army forced Washington to abandon the city and start a long and humiliating retreat. Washington and his army seemed on the brink of defeat. Then, in December 1776, Washington made a daring move. He surprised his enemy by crossing the Delaware River on Christmas night and attacking at Trenton, New Jersey. After the victory, Washington's troops did not let up. They left their campfires burning to make the enemy think they were still there. Then, they slipped away in the middle of the night to launch another surprise attack at Princeton. Washington's victories in New Jersey filled the patriots with hope that the revolution could succeed.

THE NORTHERN WAR

SARATOGA AND BENEDICT ARNOLD

Benedict Arnold

In September 1777, General Horatio Gates won praise for another key victory at **Saratoga**, New York. The victory was important because it convinced the French that the American colonists could possibly win the war. As a result, France pledged money and military support to help defeat the British. Although Gates got the credit, one of the generals under his command, **Benedict Arnold**, was the real hero of the battle. He actually led most of the fighting while Gates remained in camp. When the battle ended, Gates sent a report to Congress that did not even mention Arnold's name.

Arnold was a brave and talented commander. Along with Ethan Allen, he helped lead the attack on Fort Ticonderoga before serving under Gates's command. Despite his victories and the fact that Washington thought highly of him, Arnold grew angry as the war went on. He felt that others, like Gates, got all the credit, while his accomplishments were ignored. Finally, Arnold had enough. In 1780, he plotted to betray the Continental Army by surrendering a key location at West Point, New York. The plot failed, however, when

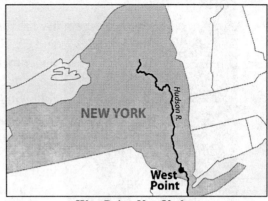

West Point, New York

patriots discovered Arnold's plan. With Washington vowing to hang his former general, Arnold fled to a British ship. He lived out his last days in England. Today, despite all he accomplished for the continental cause early in the war, Arnold is mainly remembered as a traitor.

VALLEY FORGE

Following the victory at Saratoga, the Continental Army endured a harsh winter in 1778 at **Valley Forge**, Pennsylvania. Poorly supplied and lacking warm clothes, many of Washington's men proved too sick to serve. A number of them even died. Fortunately, thanks to the efforts of Washington and a Prussian named Baron Friedrich Von Steuben, the army used its time at Valley Forge to become better trained. Once the spring arrived, Washington's army returned to battle more determined and better prepared to meet the British.

Valley Forge, Pennsylvania

THE SOUTHERN WAR

In late 1778, the British began focusing on the South. Many southerners were loyalists who the British believed would support their cause. To strengthen their effort, the British **recruited slaves**. In exchange for promises of freedom after the war, black slaves agreed to fight against the patriot forces. Eventually, some patriots responded by offering freedom as well. After the British lost the war, many of the slaves who fought for the king fled west into the frontier or south into British-held Florida. Some found freedom in other British colonies. Those same authorities who apprehended loyalist slaves returned them to slavery. As for slaves who fought with the patriots, some did receive their freedom after the war. Many, however, did not.

Slaves Fighting in the Revolution

Yorktown

General Lord Cornwallis

By the summer of 1780, the British had seized both Savannah and Charleston and were ready to bring all of the Carolinas under their control. British forces under the command of General Lord Cornwallis tried to take North Carolina following their victory at Camden. Patriots defeated them, however, at Kings Mountain and Cowpens. Eventually, Cornwallis regrouped and invaded North Carolina, pursuing General Nathanael Greene's continental forces. Cornwallis knew he had a stronger army and wanted to force Green to fight him. After leading the British on a long chase that forced Cornwallis to use up many of his supplies, Greene finally fought the British at the Battle of Guilford Courthouse. Cornwallis won, but at a heavy cost. To win the victory, he had to fire his cannons into the middle of the battle, killing many of his own men. In need of supplies, Cornwallis marched north to the coastal town of Yorktown, Virginia, where he hoped to receive help from British ships.

Realizing that Cornwallis was now trapped on the Virginia peninsula, General Washington marched south to pin him between the Continental Army and the Atlantic Ocean. Meanwhile, the French navy provided a blockade that prevented British ships from coming to Cornwallis' rescue. (A blockade is when navy ships line the coast and won't let any ships in or out.) On October 19, 1781, Cornwallis surrendered to Washington at **Yorktown**. Negotiations went on for two more years, but Yorktown effectively ended the revolution. The Americans and British finally signed the **Treaty of Paris in 1783**. The treaty ended the war, and Great Britain officially recognized the United States as an independent nation.

Surrender at Yorktown

Chapter 6

Practice 6.1: The American Revolution

1. The Stamp Act and the Townshend Acts upset colonists because they were

   A. taxes the colonists found unfair.

   B. harsh laws passed after the Boston Tea Party.

   C. part of British boycotts against American goods.

   D. meant to reduce the price of British tea.

2. Who served as the commanding general of the Continental Army and later became the first president of the United States?

   A. George Washington
   B. John Adams
   C. John Hancock
   D. George Rogers Clark

3. Benedict Arnold is most remembered as a traitor, but he was also a great commander who won key victories for the Americans at

   A. Yorktown and Bunker Hill.
   B. Lexington and Concord.
   C. Trenton and Princeton.
   D. Fort Ticonderoga and Saratoga.

4. Which of the following key figures is the only one not to serve as president of the United States?

   A. George Washington
   B. Benjamin Franklin
   C. Thomas Jefferson
   D. John Adams

6.2 THE YOUNG COUNTRY

EARLY EFFECTS OF THE REVOLUTION

Once the Continental Congress proclaimed that the colonies were independent, most states started drafting their own **state constitutions**. These constitutions were based on the same principles put forth by the Declaration of Independence. They called for **local elections** that established representative governments and guaranteed individual freedoms. Usually, white men who owned property were the only ones who could vote. However, the state of Pennsylvania opened voting to any white man over twenty-one who paid taxes. During the early days of the nation, the state constitutions actually served as

President George Washington

more powerful bodies of law than the Articles of Confederation. Most people felt they were citizens of their independent states more than they saw themselves as citizens of a new country.

Secretary of Treasury, Alexander Hamilton

One of the major problems facing the new nation after the revolution was its huge **national debt**. During the war, the United States government borrowed a lot of money from other nations and even its own citizens to pay for the revolution. The Articles of Confederation did not give the national government power to raise money and repay these debts. Some states printed cheap paper money, hurting the economy even more. Others tried to place taxes on goods bound for neighboring states, causing anger and protests. Problems like the national debt eventually led to the Constitutional Convention and the drafting of the Constitution in 1787. (Review chapter 4, section 4.1 regarding the Articles of Confederation, US Constitution, and the Bill of Rights.)

PRESIDENT GEORGE WASHINGTON

HAMILTON'S ECONOMIC PLAN

Delegates to the Electoral College unanimously elected **George Washington** the first president of the United States in 1789 and again in 1792. He was inaugurated in New York City, which served as the nation's capital for Washington's first year in office. The government then moved to Philadelphia. Congress eventually approved plans for a new capital city to be built along the Potomac River between Virginia and Maryland. President Washington himself chose the site but never lived there. The new capital was eventually named Washington, DC.

Secretary of State, Thomas Jefferson

Following his election, Washington quickly chose several men that he trusted to serve in the first presidential cabinet (review chapter 3, section 3.2 regarding the cabinet). Washington selected Thomas Jefferson to be his secretary of state and Alexander Hamilton to serve as secretary of the treasury. Hamilton quickly came up with a plan to deal with the national debt. **Hamilton's economic plan** proposed that the federal government handle paying off state debts that were largely due to the war. To raise revenue, Hamilton wanted a tax on whiskey. He reasoned that such a tax would not only raise money but would also show the power of the federal government. He also supported tariffs (taxes on imports). Not only did he believe that these tariffs would raise much needed money, he also saw them as necessary to strengthen and protect US businesses from foreign competition. Hamilton believed this was necessary to give US manufacturers a chance to succeed. Finally, Hamilton proposed establishing a **national bank**. Hamilton had a loose interpretation of the Constitution and believed that the federal government had the right to charter a bank if it was necessary to exercise its constitutional duties (in this case, coining money).

Hamilton's plan gained the support of President Washington, but it was not without controversy. Many opposed Hamilton's views, including Thomas Jefferson. Jefferson had a strict interpretation of the Constitution. Since the Constitution did not specifically state that the federal government could open a national bank, Jefferson argued that it could not. Many southerners also opposed Hamilton's plan because they were against tariffs that would lessen competition from foreign countries and raise prices on finished goods. They also feared that such measures would encourage other countries to respond with tariffs of their own. Foreign tariffs would raise the price of southern products overseas and hurt the South's economy. Finally, some of the southern states had already paid off the majority of their debts and they resented being made to help pay the debts of other states. In the end, the decision to build the new capital in the South was part of a compromise to win passage of Hamilton's economic plan.

WHISKEY REBELLION

The whiskey tax was very unpopular among farmers in western Pennsylvania, Maryland, Virginia, and North Carolina. Many of these farmers made their living converting grain into whiskey. In protest, Pennsylvania farmers launched the **Whiskey Rebellion**. They refused to pay the tax and resorted to violence. The uprising ended when President Washington organized a military force that marched into Pennsylvania and halted the resistance. The event showed that the new government had the power to enforce its laws. However, it also led many farmers and frontiersmen to see Hamilton's form of government as oppressive. More of them supported Thomas Jefferson.

The Whiskey Rebellion

George Washington

Thomas Jefferson Alexander Hamilton
Presidents Washington, Jefferson, and Hamilton

WASHINGTON AND NEUTRALITY

As the US tried to start a new government, Great Britain and France continued to fight a war against one another. President Washington knew that the young country could not afford a fight with either side. He made a **proclamation of neutrality**, in which he stated that the US would not take sides. The conflict still had consequences for the United States, however. The British began intercepting US ships they believed bound for France and impressing sailors (taking US sailors captive and forcing them to serve in the British navy). These actions were intended to injure France, but they also hurt the United States' ability to trade and operate on the high seas.

THE RISE OF POLITICAL PARTIES

Shortly before leaving office, President George Washington gave a farewell address in 1796 in which he warned against forming political parties. He believed political parties would cause people to work for special interests rather than for the public good. Despite Washington's warnings, opposing political parties did form. Men like Alexander Hamilton and John Adams led the **Federalist Party**. The Federalists supported a strong national government. They also supported tariffs and other measures meant to help US businesses. They believed the economy and the nation would do best if the government looked after the interest of manufacturers, merchants, and wealthy businessmen. Most New Englanders were Federalists. Meanwhile, the **Democratic-Republicans** arose in opposition to the Federalists. Their leaders were Thomas Jefferson and James Madison (a former Federalist). The Democratic-Republicans favored stronger state governments and a weaker national government. They tended to favor the interests of landowners, small farmers, and debtors over those of business. They opposed many Federalist policies. Most southerners and people who settled along the western frontiers were Democratic-Republicans.

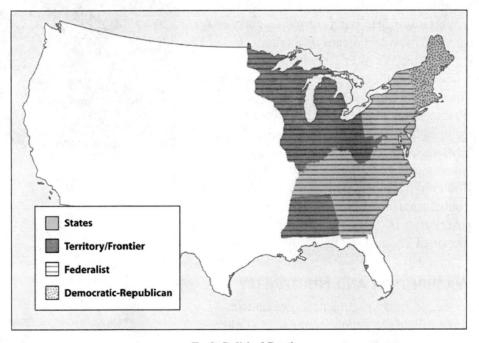

Early Political Parties

JOHN ADAMS AND THOMAS JEFFERSON

George Washington retired from public life after two terms as president. **John Adams**, his vice president, succeeded him as the nation's second president. He was a Federalist who found himself at odds with Thomas Jefferson. The Federalists in Congress passed several laws during John Adams's presidency that alarmed Jefferson and other Democratic-Republicans. The Naturalization Act required foreign immigrants to live in the United States for fourteen years before they could become US citizens. The Alien Act allowed the government to arrest and deport (force to leave the country) foreigners it viewed with suspicion. The Sedition Act limited free speech and expression (rights guaranteed under the First Amendment). Federalists often used these laws to silence critics (usually Democratic-Republicans) and prevent poor immigrants from voting. (Poorer immigrants tended to support the Democratic-Republicans over the Federalists.)

John Adams

THE ELECTION OF 1800

The battle between the Federalists and the Democratic-Republicans led to a bitter election in 1800. Jefferson's party accused Adams of wanting to be a king (a huge insult so soon after the revolution). Meanwhile, Federalists proclaimed Jefferson to be an anarchist (someone who is against any structure of government). When the Electoral College finally voted, two Democratic-Republican candidates, Thomas Jefferson and Aaron Burr, ended up tied with 73 votes each. Under the Constitution, the House of Representatives had to decide the winner. Federalist leader, Alexander Hamilton, played a major factor in deciding who won. Although Hamilton did not agree with Jefferson's politics, he hated Aaron Burr as a person. Hamilton supported Thomas Jefferson, making him the third president of the United States. Burr never forgave Hamilton for his decision and later killed him in a duel.

Burr-Hamilton Duel

Practice 6.2: The Young Country

1. Following the revolution, most states drafted their own

    A. declarations of independence.
    C. national debts.
    B. state constitutions.
    D. government banks.

2. Before the US Constitution, which of the following statements was true?
    A. The states were more powerful than the national government.
    B. The Articles of Confederation were more powerful than state constitutions.
    C. Hamilton's economic plan was rejected by many southerners.
    D. President Washington accepted the idea of a national bank.

3. A small farmer in western Georgia would have likely supported

    A. John Adams for president.
    C. the Democratic-Republicans.
    B. the Federalist Party.
    D. Hamilton's economic plan.

4. Describe the problems caused by the national debt after the war. How did the federal government end up dealing with the problem?

CHAPTER 6 REVIEW

Key Terms, People, and Concepts

Proclamation of 1763
Stamp Act
patriots
loyalists
Sons of Liberty
Townshend Acts
Boston Massacre
Committees of correspondence
Tea Act
Boston Tea Party
Intolerable Acts
Thomas Paine
Common Sense
Declaration of Independence
George Washington
Benjamin Franklin
Samuel Adams
John Adams
Thomas Jefferson

John Hancock
Patrick Henry
George Rogers Clark
Fort Ticonderoga
Saratoga
Benedict Arnold
Valley Forge
recruitment of slaves
Yorktown
Treaty of Paris, 1783
state constitutions
local elections
national debt
Hamilton's economic plan
national bank
Whiskey Rebellion
Washington's proclamation of neutrality
Federalist Party
Democratic-Republicans

Multiple Choice Questions

1. A printer in Massachusetts would have been most upset about

    A. Washington's proclamation of neutrality.

    B. the Great Compromise.

    C. the Tea Act.

    D. the Stamp Act.

2. A loyalist who refused to boycott British tea would have been most fearful of

    A. tories.

    B. British soldiers.

    C. the Sons of Liberty.

    D. the Green Mountain Boys.

3. Which person was a writer who helped win many colonists to the cause of independence during the winter of 1776?

   A. Thomas Jefferson
   B. Samuel Adams
   C. Thomas Paine
   D. George Washington.

4. Who would have been most likely to hear the speech that included these words:

   "…I know not what course others may take; but as for me, give me liberty or give me death!"

   A. a delegate at the Constitutional Convention
   B. a loyalist in Boston
   C. a soldier fighting under Benedict Arnold at Saratoga
   D. a member of the Virginia legislature

5. Benjamin Franklin's most valuable contribution to the American Revolution was his ability to
   A. negotiate a peaceful solution to differences between the colonies and Great Britain.
   B. convince the French to help.
   C. defeat the British at Valley Forge.
   D. recruit slaves to fight for the patriot cause.

6. Which of the following statements best describes Benedict Arnold?
   A. He was a great general who later turned traitor.
   B. He was a loyalist who later became a patriot.
   C. He ignited the cause of independence with the words, "…give me liberty, or give me death!"
   D. He served as the nation's first secretary of the treasury.

7. The fact that the colonies had borrowed a lot of money during the war and the increased printing of paper money after the revolution led to

   A. political parties.
   B. the call for independence.
   C. the writing of *Common Sense.*
   D. a national debt.

Look at the map below and answer the following question.

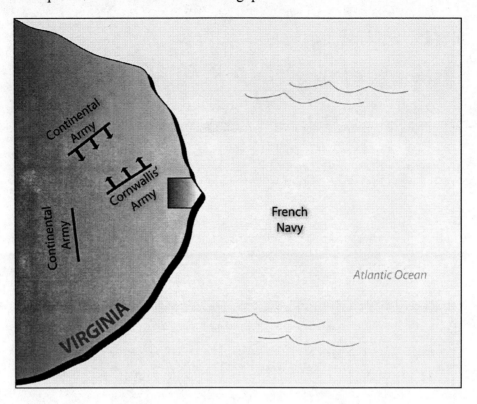

8. What battle is the map depicting?

   A. Saratoga
   B. Ticonderoga
   C. Yorktown
   D. Lexington and Concord

Chapter 7
US History: An Expanding Country

This chapter addresses the following Louisiana iLeap standard:

H-1B-M9	58. Explain Napoleon's reasons for selling the Louisiana territory to the United States and the impact of that acquisition
	59. Explain President Madison's reason for declaring war in 1812, the sectional divisions over the war, and the consequences of the Native American alliance with the British
	60. Describe provisions of the Monroe Doctrine and its influence on U.S. foreign relations
	61. Explain westward movement of the United States, the changes it created, and its effects on relations with Native Americans
	62. Explain Manifest Destiny and its economic, political, social, and religious roots
	63. Describe diplomatic and political developments that led to the resolution of conflicts with Britain, Spain, and Russia from 1815 to 1850
	64. Identify the causes, course, and consequences of the Texas War for Independence and the Mexican-American War

7.1 THE NATION MOVES WEST

OPENING THE DOOR TO EXPANSION

THE NORTHWEST TERRITORY AND LOUISIANA PURCHASE

The United States began expanding its territory soon after becoming an independent country. The land west of Pennsylvania and north of the Ohio River was known as the **Northwest Territory**. It eventually became the states of Ohio, Indiana, Illinois, Michigan, and Wisconsin. In 1803, the **Louisiana Purchase** gave the US access to vast areas of land west of the Mississippi River. (Review chapter 1, section 1.2 regarding the Ohio River Valley and Louisiana Purchase.)

US History: An Expanding Country

Legend:
- Louisiana Purchase
- Northwest Territory
- Oregon Territory
- Spanish Territory
- Claimed Territory
- United States

Territories in the Early 1800s

THE WAR OF 1812

President James Madison

As US settlers moved west, they often encountered resistance from Native Americans. Native Americans had lived in regions beyond the Ohio and Mississippi Rivers for generations. They were not happy about white settlers suddenly trying to lay claim to these lands. Many US settlers blamed the British for encouraging this resistance in order to protect their own interests in Canada. By the early 1800s, many leaders in Congress demanded war with Great Britain. They tended to represent western and southern farmers who often experienced violent conflict with Native Americans along the frontier. Meanwhile, Federalists in New England opposed the war. They represented merchants and traders in established urban areas. These merchants and traders did a great deal of business with Great Britain and other nations. They did not want their trade disrupted by an international conflict. Eventually, the "war hawks" (those in favor of war) won. **President James Madison** called for war on the grounds that Great Britain both encouraged Native American attacks against US citizens and continued to interfere with US shipping by impressing sailors. On June 18, 1812, Congress officially declared war.

Chapter 7

The **War of 1812** began with many in the US hoping to win land from the British in Canada and the Spanish in Florida (Spain was a British ally). At times, it appeared that the US was in trouble, especially when the British invaded and burned Washington, DC. New England actually considered seceding (leaving the Union) over its opposition to the war. The US persevered, however, winning an important victory at the battle of Fort McHenry. The bravery of the US soldiers who held the fort inspired Francis Scott Key to write *The Star-Spangled Banner* (today's US national anthem). Eventually, with Andrew Jackson's victory at the Battle of New Orleans, the US secured a treaty ending the war. The Treaty of Ghent did not grant any official land gains to the US, but it did keep the Mississippi River and the frontier open, encouraging further western migration. It also showed that the United States could defend itself and protect its interests. Due to its opposition to the war, the Federalist Party lost its credibility and faded from importance in national politics.

War of 1812

Sectional Differences During the War of 1812	
New England	New England's leaders opposed the war because it was bad for business. New England depended on commerce and trade with Great Britain and other nations. New Englanders did not want a war that would disrupt the economy.
South & West	Southerners and western farmers, who tended to move west, were facing violent resistance from Native Americans. Settlers believed the British were encouraging this resistance in order to prevent the US from moving west and claiming land. Southerners and westerners supported the war because they believed it was necessary to get rid of the British before they could end Native American opposition to westward expansion.

THE MONROE DOCTRINE

After the War of 1812 and the end of the Federalist Party, the United States entered a period of national pride and political unity known as the Era of Good Feelings. It was during this period that President James Monroe issued the **Monroe Doctrine** in 1823. Monroe proclaimed that the United States would not tolerate European intervention in the Western Hemisphere (North and South America). He also declared that the American continents were no longer open to European colonization. The US would view any future attempts at colonization as threats. Finally, the president promised that the United States would not interfere in the affairs of other countries. In reality, the US was not militarily prepared to enforce Monroe's stances. Fortunately for the president,

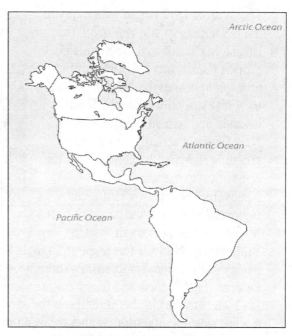

Map of the Western Hemisphere

however, Great Britain backed the policy for economic reasons. Britain used its powerful navy to keep routes of trade open and discourage any European intervention in the Americas.

THE OREGON TRAIL

In the early 1800s, Great Britain, the United States, Russia, and Spain all claimed portions of the **Oregon Territory** (region that now makes up the northwest United States and parts of southwestern Canada). None of the four countries gave any consideration to the Native Americans who had lived in the region for centuries. In 1818, the US and Great Britain signed a treaty agreeing to share custody of the land. Soon afterwards, Russia and Spain withdrew their claims. (See next section entitled "Relations with Spain.")

The Oregon Trail

Following the Lewis and Clark Expedition (review chapter 1, section 1.2), more settlers headed west. Mountain men soon lived throughout the Oregon Territory, opening paths for those who would come after them. Some settlers migrated west for land. Others searched for gold. A number of missionaries moved west to convert Native Americans to Christianity. Eventually, a number of trails developed. These trails were simply well-traveled routes used by settlers to head west. Perhaps the most famous was the **Oregon Trail**. The Oregon Trail started in Independence, Missouri, and ran west into the Oregon Territory.

Pioneers on the Oregon Trail

Thanks to the Oregon Trail, the Oregon Territory became home to a growing number of US citizens. As the territory's population grew, so did cries for the United States government to lay claim to the entire region.

RELATIONS WITH SPAIN

Map of Florida

Secretary of State, John Quincy Adams

In 1817, conflict arose between white settlers and Native Americans along the Georgia-Florida frontier. The president responded by ordering his famed military leader, Andrew Jackson, to put an end to the fighting. Without permission, Jackson went further and tried to drive the Spanish out of Florida. Secretary of State John Quincy Adams supported Jackson's aggressive actions. He told Spain that if it could not maintain order in Florida, then it should cede the land to the United States. In 1819, Spain and the United States signed the **Adams-Onis Treaty**. Under the treaty, Spain ceded Florida and any claim it laid to the Oregon Territory to the US. In return, the United States gave up any claim to the Texas Territory and agreed to a border between the Louisiana Territory and Spanish territory in the North American southwest.

Manifest Destiny

Manifest Destiny

As the United States approached the middle of the nineteenth century, many leaders and citizens believed it was God's will for the US to expand west. They felt that white Americans were destined to spread "civilized democracy" and possess territory all the way to the Pacific Ocean. People who shared this belief considered it the nation's destiny to conquer the West. Their ideology became known as **Manifest Destiny**.

Texas: Independence and Annexation

In 1821, Mexico gained independence from Spain. Mexico also gained control of Texas. **Texas** was home to a large number of US settlers. In 1834, General Antonio Santa Anna assumed power over the Mexican government and tightened his control over Texas. In response, Texans under the leadership of Sam Houston launched a rebellion. On March 2, 1836, a convention of Texas delegates declared the territory to be an independent republic. Santa Anna answered with military force. On March 6, a small group of Texans took their stand against the Mexican leader at an old

The Alamo

mission called **The Alamo**. Despite the Texans' brave resistance, Santa Anna's forces were too strong. Every Texan who fought at the Alamo died in the battle or was executed after being captured (among them, the famed Davy Crockett of Tennessee). After a series of battles, the Texans defeated Santa Anna and took him hostage. In exchange for his freedom, the Mexican leader promised to give up Texas. Wanting to become part of the United States, Texans asked to be annexed (made part of the US). President Andrew Jackson wanted to annex Texas, but northerners in Congress did not. Because of its southern location, northerners knew that Texas would be admitted as a slave state. They also feared that, because of its large size, the area might be divided into *several* slave states. If this happened, it would give slave states an advantage in Congress. Texas remained an independent nation until 1845.

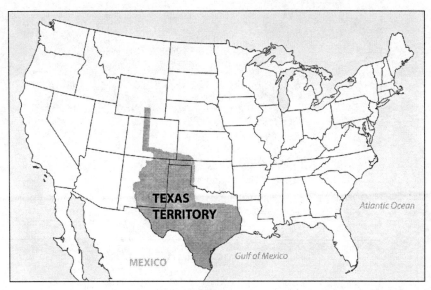

Texas Territory

Whether or not to annex Texas was a critical issue in the election of 1844. James Polk took a strong stand as the Democratic candidate for president. He called for the annexation of both Texas and Oregon. Polk's election inspired his predecessor, President John Tyler, to call on Congress to pass a resolution admitting Texas to the Union as a slave state. Congress finally agreed, and Texas became a state in 1845.

OREGON

With the question of Texas settled, Polk turned his attention to annexing the Oregon Territory. President Polk approached Britain, arguing that the US had rightful claim to the territory up to 54°40'N latitude. Polk's aggressive tone irritated the British, but they were ready to give up Oregon because the territory was no longer profitable. The United States had also become an important consumer of British goods, leading Britain to want friendly terms with the US. The United States accepted a treaty declaring 49°N latitude the official boundary. In 1846, Oregon became a US territory.

President James Polk

US History: An Expanding Country

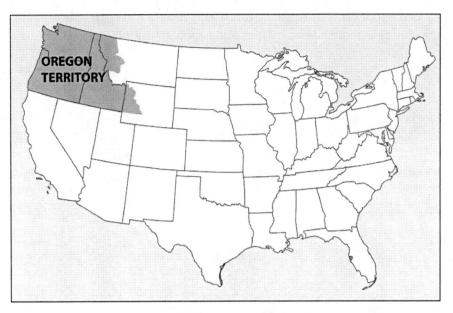

Map of the Oregon Territory

WAR WITH MEXICO AND THE GADSDEN PURCHASE

Mexico was angry with the US for annexing Texas. However, this did not deter President Polk and leaders in Congress who believed in Manifest Destiny. In June 1845, Polk ordered US troops to the Texas border. He also sent a Louisiana businessman and politician, John Slidell, to Mexico. Polk wanted Slidell to settle disputes over the boundary between the United States and Mexico. Polk hoped to get treaty that would allow the US to purchase the California and New Mexico territories. After the

War with Mexico

Mexican president refused to meet with Slidell, Polk ordered US troops to move into the disputed territory. In response, Mexican troops crossed the Rio Grande and attacked Taylor's forces. Immediately, Polk demanded that Congress declare war on Mexico. He claimed that the Mexicans had "shed American blood on American soil." Though some representatives doubted Polk's claim, Congress passed a declaration of war on May 13, 1846. The war was a series of US victories leading up to September 14, 1847, when General Winfield Scott marched his troops into Mexico City and forced Mexico to surrender. After months of negotiations, the US and Mexico finally ended the war with the Treaty of Guadalupe-Hidalgo on February 2, 1848. The treaty required Mexico to sell the New Mexico and California territories to the United States.

John Slidell   James Gadsden

In 1853, boundary disputes with Mexico still remained. President Franklin Pierce sent James Gadsden to settle the problem and to purchase land for a southern transcontinental railroad. The **Gadsden Purchase** gave the United States parts of present-day New Mexico and Arizona in exchange for ten million dollars. The purchase of these areas finalized the expanse of the continental United States to the present day.

CALIFORNIA

In 1848, settlers discovered gold just north of Sacramento, California. The following year, gold seekers came from all over the world as part of the California **Gold Rush** of 1849. These new arrivals were called "49ers," and they rapidly increased California's population. This growth produced a need for stable government almost overnight. After much debate over whether or not to allow slavery in the territory, Congress voted to admit California as a free state in 1850. Gold drew settlers west to other regions as well. (Review chapter 1, section 1.2.)

California 49ers

FEDERAL LEGISLATION

In order to fulfill Manifest Destiny, the nation needed citizens who were willing to move west. To encourage migration, the federal government passed several laws. The **Preemption Act** of 1841 stated that citizens who had lived on a particular piece of land for at least fourteen months could purchase up to 160 acres at a reduced price before the land was sold to the public. The law also promised partial reimbursements of the proceeds to some western territories once they became states (Louisiana was among them). The law encouraged people to move west and establish homesteads in hopes of eventually purchasing the land for very little. Later, the

Western Farmer in the Mid 1800s

Homestead Act of 1862 granted ownership of land to those willing to cultivate at least 160 acres for five years. The **Morrill-Land Grant Act**, passed the same year, gave certain western territories to state governments. These governments could then sell the land in order to raise money to establish colleges that would specialize in teaching new farming methods. The Morrill-Land Grant Act increased the western population as it trained a new generation of farmers to tackle the rough terrain of the North American west.

Practice 7.1: The Nation Moves West

1. The route taken by settlers heading west from Missouri into what is today the northwest corner of the United States was known as the

   A. Oregon Trail.
   B. Manifest Trail.
   C. Manifest Destiny.
   D. Gadsden Route.

2. Manifest Destiny was the

   A. route most settlers took as they headed west.
   B. name of the mission President Pierce gave to James Gadsden.
   C. belief that the United States should conquer and claim the West.
   D. belief that it was God's will for Texas to declare independence from Mexico.

3. The Preemption Act was intended to

   A. limit western migration.
   B. increase western migration.
   C. force Mexico to surrender territory to the US or go to war.
   D. encourage states to open new colleges.

Chapter 7

7.2 THE IMPACT OF TECHNOLOGY AND INFRASTRUCTURE

HENRY CLAY'S AMERICAN SYSTEM

Clay supported several measures he thought were crucial to improving the nation's economy.

Henry Clay

1. **Protective tariff** (a tax on imports): The American System called for a tariff to help US manufacturing continue to grow and compete with other nations. During the War of 1812, US manufacturing grew and improved because the US could not trade with Great Britain and other European powers. Once the war ended, however, US manufacturers once again had to compete against foreign producers.

2. **Internal improvements**: Clay called for better canals, roadways, and railways. He believed construction should be funded by the federal government's tariff revenue. By improving transportation, different US regions could engage in trade with one another much easier. Clay argued it would unite the country, increase a sense of nationalism (pride in one's country), and lessen the United States' dependence on foreign countries.

3. **A Strong National Bank**: Alexander Hamilton's first national bank no longer existed because its charter (document giving it the legal right to exist) had expired. Without a national bank, states issued their own money. This made it very difficult for states to trade. People traveling from one state to another often found themselves with money they could not easily use. Clay believed a national bank was necessary to make sure everyone used the same kind of paper money, making interstate commerce easier, and strengthening the economy.

Clay, however, underestimated the nation's growing **sectionalism**. Sectionalism refers to the differences that divide people by region. Southerners tended to believe that the federal government should restrict itself to powers specifically stated in the Constitution. They favored more power for the states. Many southern leaders believed that they could refuse to enforce federal laws they saw as unconstitutional or harmful. Northerners were more prone to support a strong central government. Southerners opposed tariffs like those proposed by Clay because they raised the price on manufactured imports and invited other countries to impose tariffs of their own. Such actions hurt the South's ability to sell cotton and other agricultural products overseas. Northerners, however, supported tariffs because they made imports more expensive. The more expensive imports, the more attractive US products were to consumers. Clay's national bank had problems also. Many small landowners distrusted the bank. They blamed it for economic problems that faced small farmers.

Cumberland Road and the Erie Canal

The Cumberland Road

The Erie Canal

As white Americans moved west, the need to improve infrastructure increased. **Infrastructure** is what provides the framework and connections for holding something together. For instance, in a country like the United States, infrastructure includes roads, rail lines, canals (canals are man-made waterways meant to make travel faster and easier), and so forth. In 1811, the federal government began construction on the **Cumberland Road**. The road began at Cumberland, Maryland, and by 1819 extended through Virginia to the Ohio River. Construction continued with the intent to run the road all the way to St. Louis, Missouri. When funding ran out, however, the Cumberland Road (also called the National Road) stopped in Illinois. The road helped make travel much easier and opened the way for more people to travel west.

The government completed another major project in 1825. The **Erie Canal** provided a new shipping route from Lake Erie to the Hudson River. Because it connected New York City to the Great Lakes, the canal expanded New York's markets and made the city a major commercial center. It also allowed people to travel much cheaper, carrying their household goods with them. Whole families could move west easier than before. Along with Robert Fulton's invention of the **steamboat** (boat powered by steam), the Erie Canal boosted the economy of New York City and the northeastern United States.

Robert Fulton

Important Technology

The Cotton Gin

Eli Whitney

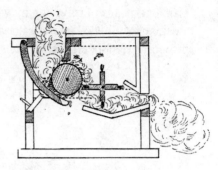

The Cotton Gin

Important new technology accompanied the nation's expansion. One of the earliest to have impact was Eli Whitney's **cotton gin**. Whitney's machine allowed people to process harvested cotton much faster and made the South a "cotton kingdom" (economically dependent on cotton). Many southern plantation owners got rich as people in both the US and overseas demanded more cotton. As the cotton gin led to a boom in cotton plantations, the South became very dependent on slave labor. The invention also encouraged western migration. People moved west in hopes of raising cotton and earning their fortune. The cotton gin and other agricultural inventions helped fuel support for slavery in new US territories in the years after the War of 1812.

The Steel and Mechanical Plow

Farmer Using Steel Plow

The terrain of the Great Plains and the Midwest proved to be much harder than that of the eastern United States. Farmers could not rely on the same old equipment and methods to grow crops. Without new inventions, agriculture would have been difficult, and people could not have migrated west in great numbers. John Deere introduced his **steel plow** in the 1830s. The steel plow allowed farmers to cut through the tough prairie sod of the Midwest and plant seed in the fertile ground beneath. Later, **mechanical plows** allowed farmers to plow more territory faster. Thanks to such inventions, the Midwest eventually became known as the "Breadbasket of America." Today, it supplies a large portion of the United States' agricultural supply and much of the farm produce that feeds the rest of the world.

THE STEAMBOAT

As mentioned earlier, the **steamboat** proved to be an important invention. Previously, boats had to be powered manually, or they relied on sails. People could only paddle so fast, and sails left crews and passengers at the mercy of the wind. Steamboats provided a much faster and more efficient means of traveling by water. Coupled with canals and available river routes, steamboats allowed interstate trade and commerce to increase and contributed to expansion by providing a more efficient means of transportation.

Steamboat

RAILROADS

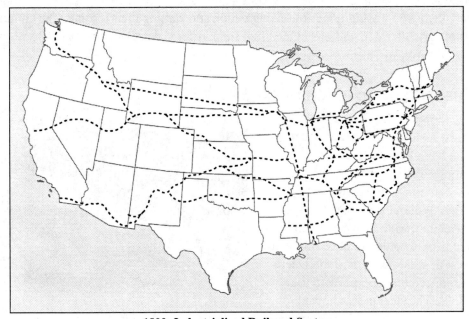
1800s Industrialized Railroad System

As the 1800s progressed, the US continued to expand and become more and more industrialized. **Railroads** played a major role in this industrial growth and expansion. Railroads contributed to the rise of the steel industry and big business. In the 1850s, a man named Henry Bessemer developed a new method for making steel, known as the Bessemer process. Using this process, manufacturers could make steel much cheaper. As a result, steel became more affordable, leading to faster expansion of railroads and more construction. Thanks to steel, buildings could be constructed taller than ever before. By building taller buildings, cities like New York could hold more people and industry even though land was limited. Steel became very important to the nation's economy.

1800s Railroad Engine

Before railroads, most goods had to be transported by water. You couldn't load something like steel beams on wagons and transport them over land very easily. Even if you tried, you would not be able to haul very much. Water was the only way to transport large amounts of heavy products. Unfortunately, shipping products by water meant that you had to follow the route of the river you were navigating. Goods could only reach certain areas and a limited number of people. Railroads changed this. Since railroads were much larger and faster than wagons, they became a practical and economical way to ship large products over land. Because of their ability to carry goods and resources great distances, railroads became important to the growth of big business.

Western Cowboy

Railroads also made life in the West easier. They allowed farmers, ranchers, and other settlers access to eastern markets and resources. Railroads opened a way for farmers to import needed equipment from the East while shipping their own products to different parts of the country. Meanwhile, western cattle ranchers could drive their cattle to "cowtowns." **Cowtowns** were western towns that formed mainly as a place where ranchers could load their cattle on trains and ship them east to market. Thanks to railroads, farmers and ranchers could settle in western territories without being totally isolated.

Railroads also made it easier for people to move west and populate territories at a rapid rate. In 1862, Congress coordinated an effort among the railroad companies to build a **Transcontinental Railroad**. Union Pacific (an eastern rail company) and Central Pacific (a rail company from Sacramento, California) joined their tracks at Promontory, Utah, in 1869. As a symbol of their union that linked the nation east to west, representatives drove a gold spike to join the tracks.

Promontory, Utah

US History: An Expanding Country

Practice 7.2: The Impact of Technology and Infrastructure

1. In order to better unite the nation, Henry Clay proposed
   - A. more state banks.
   - B. many forms of currency.
   - C. an end to tariffs.
   - D. a second national bank.

2. A merchant in New York City would have been **most** excited about the
   - A. invention of the steel plow.
   - B. completion of the Erie Canal.
   - C. building of the Cumberland Road.
   - D. cotton gin.

3. Describe the impact of railroads on the growth of business and western expansion.

7.3 EFFECTS OF EXPANSION ON NATIVE AMERICANS

BUFFALO AND RESERVATIONS

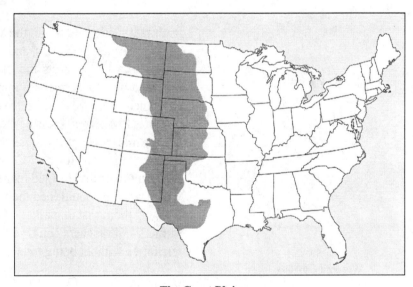

The Great Plains

As settlers ventured west, Native Americans felt the impact. For instance, the **Great Plains** had long provided many Native Americans with their livelihood. (Review chapter 1, section 1.2 regarding the Great Plains.) The buffalo, in particular, provided food, clothing, and shelter. As settlers and fur trappers came into the region, they killed great numbers of buffalo for their hides and to make way for ranchers' herds of cattle. Railroads both disturbed the natural environment of the Great Plains and rapidly increased the number of US citizens migrating into the territory. By 1889, only 1,000 buffalo were left on the continent. As a result, the Plains Indians could no longer continue their way of life. In addition, many Native American tribes were forced to

Buffalo

Plains Indians

relocate to **reservations**. Reservations were parcels of land set aside by the federal government for Native Americans. Time and again, Native Americans were forced to move, only to be relocated each time gold was discovered or whites wanted land. Large numbers of Native Americans died as a result of being forced to travel great distances. Over time, many Native Americans grew bitter, leading to wars between whites and Native Americans.

VIOLENT CONFRONTATIONS

SAND CREEK

Often, Native Americans chose to resist white settlement rather than accept being moved. In 1861, the Cheyenne grew angry after being forced off of land promised to them by the US government. Cheyenne warriors launched several raids on mining camps and local settlements, killing white settlers. In response, US forces surprised 500 Cheyenne at Sand Creek, massacring roughly 270 Native Americans, most of whom were women and children.

LITTLE BIGHORN

When news of Sand Creek spread, other Native American tribes became enraged. Under the leadership of chiefs Red Cloud and Crazy Horse, the Sioux Indians rose up. In 1876, a US commander named George Armstrong Custer attempted to surprise the Sioux at the Battle of the Little Bighorn. Custer greatly underestimated the size of his enemy's forces, however, and recklessly rushed into battle. Sioux warriors quickly surrounded the outnumbered US troops. They killed Custer and more than

Red Cloud

Crazy Horse

200 of his men. The battle became known as "Custer's last stand." It was the last great victory for Native Americans over federal troops. By 1877, both the Sioux and Cheyenne had surrendered and been forcibly moved to reservations in the Dakotas and Oklahoma.

Chief Joseph

The Nez Perce were a tribe led by Chief Joseph. When the US government attempted to remove them from the Oregon Territory, violence broke out. Several Nez Perce warriors killed white settlers without Chief Joseph's blessing. Hoping to avoid further bloodshed, Joseph ordered that the tribe obey US orders to move to a northern reservation. On the way, federal troops attacked the tribe. Chief Joseph then began a masterful retreat in which he outmaneuvered his pursuers for several months. His goal was to reach Canada. US forces stopped the Nez Perce thirty miles from the border, however, and forced them to settle on reservations in Oklahoma. The Nez Perce almost died out as many of them suffered from sickness and malnutrition.

Chief Joseph

Wounded Knee

Wounded Knee, South Dakota

The last notable armed conflict between US troops and Native Americans occurred in 1890 at **Wounded Knee**. A Sioux holy man named Wovoka developed a religious ritual called the Ghost Dance. The Sioux believed that this dance would bring back the buffalo and return the Native American tribes to their land. US officials believed that the Sioux leader, Sitting Bull, was using the Ghost Dance to start a Native American uprising. The government sent in the US army to arrest Sitting Bull and put a stop to the Ghost Dance movement. A gunfight erupted, resulting in the deaths of fourteen people, including Sitting Bull himself. Soldiers then pursued the Sioux to Wounded Knee Creek. When a shot rang out (no one is sure who fired it), the soldiers started shooting. Before it was over, more than 150 Native American men, women, and children lay dead.

Ghost Dance

Sitting Bull

Chapter 7

THE DAWES ACT

In 1887, Congress passed the **Dawes Act**. The government intended to use the law to assimilate Native Americans into white culture. It ended tribal organizations and divided up reservations for the purpose of giving land to individual Native American families. After twenty-five years, ownership of the land would go to the Native Americans and they would become US citizens. Unfortunately, the Dawes Act turned out to be a huge failure. Most Native Americans did not want to give up their tribal identity. Many had no interest in farming or becoming like white Americans. Even those who wished to farm often were given land not suitable for growing crops. Many Native Americans fell victim to crooked federal officials who cheated them out of land and money. In the end, the Dawes Act accomplished little as the Native American population decreased due to poverty and disease.

Practice 7.3: Effects of Expansion on Native Americans

1. The United States government's approach to dealing with Native Americans can best be described as

    A. cooperative because it respected Native Americans.

    B. passive because it showed little interests in invading Native American lands.

    C. aggressive because the government was willing to use force to take Native American lands.

    D. fair because the government would not take any land without first agreeing to pay Native Americans what it was worth.

2. How did cattle ranching and railroads affect Native Americans of the Great Plains?

3. What was the purpose of reservations?

4. What did the Dawes Act state, why was it passed, and how effective was it?

US History: An Expanding Country

CHAPTER 7 REVIEW

Key Terms, People, and Concepts

Northwest Territory
Louisiana Purchase
President James Madison
War of 1812
sectional differences during the War of 1812
Monroe Doctrine
Oregon Territory
Oregon Trail
Adams-Onis Treaty
Manifest Destiny
Texas
the Alamo
War with Mexico
Gadsden Purchase
gold rush
Preemption Act
Homestead Act
Morrill-Land Grant Act

American System
protective tariff
Second National Bank
sectionalism
infrastructure

Cumberland Road
Erie Canal
steamboat
cotton gin
steel and mechanical plows
railroads
cowtowns
Transcontinental Railroad
Great Plains
reservations
Wounded Knee
Dawes Act

Multiple Choice Questions

1. Early in the United States' history, the nation began to expand. The new territories it claimed north of the Ohio River and west of Pennsylvania were known as the

   A. the Northwest Territory.
   B. the Oregon Territory.
   C. the Louisiana Territory.
   D. Texas.

Look at the map below and answer the following question.

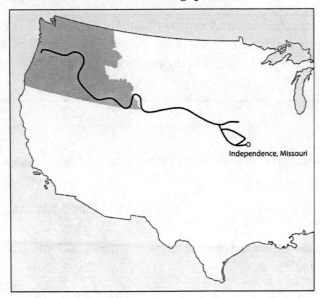

2. The map above depicts
   A. the Alamo.
   B. the Gadsden Purchase.
   C. the Oregon Trail.
   D. land the US bought from Mexico.

Using the same map as #2, answer the following question.

3. The shaded territory in the map is the
   A. California Territory.
   B. Louisiana Territory.
   C. Oregon Territory.
   D. Northwest Territory.

4. Arthur is a representative to Congress in 1812. He strongly opposes any war with Great Britain because he fears it would disrupt trade and hurt US business. Arthur most likely represents citizens
   A. living along the frontier.
   B. in western Georgia.
   C. who are war hawks.
   D. in New England.

US History: An Expanding Country

> "We are called by our Almighty Creator to head west. It is His will that we subdue the savage, conquer the wilderness, and carry the Christian banner and civility to all corners of the continent!"
>
> US Congressman 1846

5. The Congressman who made the above quote clearly believed in
   A. the Monroe Doctrine.
   B. war with Great Britain.
   C. Manifest Destiny.
   D. the American System.

6. Which of the following opened the way west by providing an open path from Maryland to Illinois?
   A. the Erie Canal
   B. the Cumberland Road
   C. the Oregon Trail
   D. the Louisiana Purchase

7. Which of the following statements best describes the effects of white westward expansion on most Native Americans?
   A. White expansion helped Native Americans because it introduced new technology and ideas about government.
   B. White expansion hurt Native Americans because it drove them from their lands and resulted in death, poverty, and the destruction of their way of life.
   C. As whites moved west it initially hurt Native Americans who had to move to reservations. Later, however, it helped Native Americans because many of them eventually grew wealthy thanks to the Dawes Act.
   D. White expansion had little effect until gold was discovered; then it hurt Native Americans because they did not know how to convert their gold to money.

8. Due to new technologies like railroads, the cotton gin, and John Deere's steel plow, farmers and ranchers
   A. were unable to survive in the West.
   B. were able to farm and ranch without bothering Native Americans.
   C. thrived in the West.
   D. found themselves losing land to big businesses located in cowtowns.

Chapter 8
Democracy, Religion, and Reform

This chapter addresses the following Louisiana iLeap standards:

H-1B-M10	65. Describe Jacksonian democracy, the influence of Jackson on the U.S. political system, and Jackson's Indian Removal Policy
	66. Identify major technological developments related to land, water, and transportation and explain how they transformed the economy, created international markets, and affected the environment
	67. Analyze national policies on a protective tariff, a national bank, federally funded improvements (e.g., roads, canals, railroads), and educational and prison reforms
	68. Compare ways of life in northern and southern states and identify factors that caused rapid urbanization and the growth of slavery
	69. Identify the causes and explain the effects of new waves of immigration prior to the Civil War
H-1B-M11	70. Explain the importance of the Second Great Awakening, the ideas of its principal leaders, and how it affected public education, temperance, woman's suffrage, and abolition
	71. Describe fundamental beliefs of abolitionists and compare positions of those who favored gradual versus immediate emancipation
	72. Identify the major antebellum reform movements, their leaders, and the movements' effects on the United States

8.1 JACKSONIAN DEMOCRACY

Andrew Jackson was a war hero and a "common man." He was not born into the rich upper class. Instead, he achieved his success despite growing up poor and uneducated. As a result, he was very popular with western frontier settlers and "common folk." In 1824, he decided to take advantage of his popularity and run for president.

Andrew Jackson

Democracy, Religion, and Reform

A "Corrupt Bargain"

John Quincy Adams

More than any previous election, the presidential election of 1824 showed the sectional differences in the United States. New England backed the current secretary of state, John Quincy Adams. (Adams' father was John Adams, the nation's second president.) Southerners supported William Crawford of Georgia. Both Henry Clay and Andrew Jackson represented western interests. The election came down to a choice between Adams and Jackson. It was so close that the House of Representatives had to decide the winner. When Clay threw his support to Adams, it gave Jackson's opponent the victory. Jackson and his followers soon protested when they learned that Clay would be named secretary of state. Jackson denounced the election as a "corrupt bargain" between Adams and Clay. Four years later, Jackson defeated Adams to become the nation's president.

Universal (White Male) Suffrage

Common Folk

Jackson's brand of politics and the changes he inspired came to be called **Jacksonian Democracy**. Jackson believed strongly in western expansion and the rights of white frontier settlers. He, like many westerners, resented "eastern elites" and political leaders who seemed to favor the upper class. Jackson favored **universal suffrage**. In other words, he believed that all white men should be free to vote, not just those who owned property. Due to the efforts of men like Jackson, all but a few states dropped property requirements for voting. Expanding suffrage made the nation more democratic and enabled "simpler men" to hold positions of power in government. (It is important to remember, however, that even Jacksonian Democracy did not attempt to give women, blacks, or Native Americans the right to vote.)

The "Spoils System," Strict Interpretation, and Laissez-Faire Economics

Spoils System

Once in office, Jackson instituted a policy of rewarding his political supporters with government positions. This policy became known as the **spoils system**, and it set a precedent for rewarding

The Spoils System

faithful supporters with government jobs. Jackson believed it was a great way to encourage common people to become politically involved. He also felt it would ensure that wealthy politicians did not control the government. The spoils system eventually led to corruption and a call for reform in later presidencies.

LAISSEZ-FAIRE ECONOMICS

Jackson and his followers also favored **laissez-faire economics**. They did not think the government should regulate business or pass policies to help US businessmen (although Jackson did occasionally support tariffs, so long as he did not think they hurt small farmers). Jackson believed that such measures tended to favor wealthy easterners while hurting southern farmers and landowners along the western frontier. Jackson did not want to hurt US businesses, but he did want to make sure smaller merchants and small landowners had as much chance to succeed as wealthy citizens.

Andrew Jackson

STRICT INTERPRETATION

Jackson also had a **strict interpretation** of the Constitution. Though his enemies accused him of acting more like a king than a president, Andrew Jackson believed that the federal government should be restricted to only those powers specifically stated in the Constitution. As a result, he used all the power at his disposal to close the second national bank during his second term in office. He believed the bank favored rich elites. Like Thomas Jefferson before him, he also pointed out that the Constitution gave the government no power to establish a bank. Unfortunately, Jackson's actions contributed to a nationwide depression in 1837.

THE KITCHEN CABINET

Picture Mocking "The Kitchen Cabinet"

President Jackson relied more on the advice of an unofficial group of advisors than he did on his official presidential cabinet. It was made up of longtime friends and political allies. Jackson's opponents referred to this group as the president's **Kitchen Cabinet**. Many politicians resented the Kitchen Cabinet. They believed the president's top advisors should only be those holding official posts. They also looked down on its members, seeing them as ignorant, uneducated men like the president. Jackson, however, viewed his unofficial cabinet as a way to include "common men" whom he trusted in the political process.

INDIAN REMOVAL

Trail of Tears

Andrew Jackson believed in Manifest Destiny. He saw the Native Americans that occupied western territories as an obstacle to expansion. As a result, he supported **Indian Removal**. Under this policy, the US government forced Native Americans off lands it wanted for white settlement. Perhaps the most famous example of Jackson's support for this policy was his refusal to help the Cherokee in north Georgia and the western Carolinas. Despite the fact that the Cherokee had helped him during the War of 1812, Jackson supported Georgia's efforts to remove the tribe during the 1830s. Georgia's government wanted Cherokee territory for the land, resources, and gold it offered. When the Supreme Court ruled that the Cherokee had the right to keep their land, white Georgians ignored the decision and continued claiming Native American territory. When the Cherokee appealed to Jackson to uphold the Supreme Court's decision, the president voiced his belief that the Court had acted outside of its constitutional powers. Jackson sarcastically stated that since it was Chief Justice John Marshall's decision, he could enforce it. Jackson's lack of concern for Native Americans led to the forced removal of the Cherokee in 1838. Their march west to Oklahoma became known as the **Trail of Tears** because of the many Cherokee who suffered and died along the way.

THE BATTLE OVER FEDERAL POWER

Jackson's strict interpretation of the Constitution meant that he often tried to limit federal power. He did not want the federal government passing laws and practicing policies he viewed as unfair to common citizens. However, when Jackson was convinced that an act of the national government was constitutional, he did his best to uphold it. As a result, Jackson eventually made a number of enemies.

Andrew Jackson

SOUTH CAROLINA NULLIFICATION CRISIS

During the mid-1800s, leaders still debated over which had more power: the federal or state governments. Jackson believed that the federal government had limited powers but that its authority was greater than that of the states. Once a federal law was passed by Congress, Jackson believed the states were bound to obey it. Many politicians disagreed. Even Jackson's own vice president, John C. Calhoun, opposed him. The split was so serious that Calhoun resigned as vice president so he could return to the US Senate to represent South Carolina. The differences between the two men resulted in the **South Carolina Nullification Crisis**. The crisis arose in 1832 when South Carolina began protesting high tariffs. State leaders claimed that South Carolina had the right to refuse to obey any law it deemed unconstitutional. Such a belief is known as the **doctrine of nullification** because it holds that states can *nullify* any federal law they feel violates the Constitution. South Carolina based its claim on a pamphlet written by Calhoun in 1828. In his pamphlet, entitled *Exposition and Protest*, Calhoun argued for **states' rights** (the idea that, to a great extent, states should be allowed to govern themselves). He asserted that any state could refuse to enforce a law it saw as unconstitutional. In 1832, South Carolina threatened to exercise this right and secede from the Union if Congress did not repeal the tariffs. Enraged, Jackson threatened to hang Calhoun personally. He also prepared to use federal troops to force South Carolina to obey the law. Finally, Senator Henry Clay proposed a compromise both sides could accept. Clay's compromise ended the South Carolina nullification crisis, but the issues of states' rights and secession remained alive until the end of the Civil War.

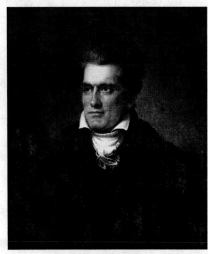

John C. Calhoun

RETURN OF THE TWO-PARTY SYSTEM

Martin Van Buren

Cartoon Mocking King Andrew

Sharp differences over the government's role in the economy and development led to a break in the Democratic-Republican Party. Jackson's wing took the name "Democrats" while his opponents adopted the name "National Republicans." Many of the National Republicans later formed a new party, the "Whigs." They chose the name "Whigs" because it was the name of the British party that opposed King George III during the Revolutionary War. Since they accused Jackson of acting like "King Andrew," they adopted the same name. After an "era of good feelings," the **two-party system** returned to national politics.

Jackson left office after his second term. His vice president and fellow Democrat, Martin Van Buren, became the next president in 1836. Interestingly, Van Buren's presidential campaign gave birth to the common expression, "O.K." It originally stood for "Old Kinderhook," Van Buren's nickname. However, Andrew Jackson's enemies in the Whig Party turned it around and used it to mock the president's lack of education. They said the initials stood for the way Jackson use to approve executive papers, simply writing "o.k." They claimed it stood for the term "oll korrect": Jackson's way of spelling "all correct."

Practice 8.1: Jacksonian Democracy

1. Andrew Jackson introduced a brand of politics known as
    A. the Kitchen Cabinet.
    B. a Corrupt Bargain.
    C. King Andrew.
    D. Jacksonian Democracy.

2. Why did many political opponents criticize the Kitchen Cabinet?
    A. They felt it was inappropriate for the president to meet with his official advisors in the White House kitchen.
    B. They resented a bunch of "uneducated" and unofficial advisors taking the place of the actual cabinet.
    C. Many opponents were National Republicans, while most of the members of the Kitchen Cabinet were Whigs.
    D. Critics felt too many members of the Kitchen Cabinet were eastern elites; they wanted to see more common men given positions of leadership.

3. Who did Andrew Jackson believe should have the right to vote in the US?
    A. all white males
    B. all white males who owned sufficient property
    C. all citizens regardless of race or gender
    D. all white people

4. How did Jackson's belief in the power of the federal government over that of the states contribute to the South Carolina Nullification Crisis?

8.2 RELIGION AND REFORM

THE SECOND GREAT AWAKENING

During the early 1700s, the North American colonies experienced a time of religious revival. Preachers traveled about delivering fiery sermons and calling people to a sincere faith. They challenged many traditional Protestant and Catholic views that placed importance on religious ceremonies. Instead, these preachers emphasized understanding and applying biblical principles and rejected ceremonial worship. This period became known as the First Great Awakening. During the first half of the 1800s, the US

The Second Great Awakening

experienced another revival. This movement became known as the **Second Great Awakening**. Once again, zealous preachers traveled from place to place inspiring people with religious enthusiasm. Often they preached in meetings held outside, called "tent meetings" or "revivals." They emphasized a personal commitment to God through the Gospel of Jesus Christ and taught that, through the good works of believers, society could be changed for the better. This religious zeal became the motivation behind many people's involvement in social causes. Thanks partly to the Second Great Awakening, a number of important **reform movements** (movements meant to make society better) arose during the 1800s.

REFORM MOVEMENTS

EDUCATIONAL REFORM

The first public schools appeared in New England during the 1640s. After the American Revolution, the United States began to use education as a way of promoting nationalism and unity. In the 1830s, a reformer named **Horace Mann** greatly impacted US education. Mann believed in the education of both men and women through public schools. He felt that education was essential to the success of democracy. Mann helped create the state Board of Education in Massachusetts. Soon, his ideas spread across the nation. By 1870, every state in the Union provided some form of free public education.

Democracy, Religion, and Reform

Horace Mann

Public School in the Mid 1800s

PRISON AND MENTAL HEALTH REFORM

Dorothea Dix

In the 1800s, states began building prisons for the purpose of rehabilitation (helping prisoners become law-abiding citizens). Before this time, those who committed crimes were physically punished. Authorities often flogged (beat) convicted criminals, or publicly humiliated them by locking them in public stocks. **Dorothea Dix** became a great advocate for both **prison reform** (improving the treatment of prisoners) and the rights of the mentally disabled. In 1841, Dix visited a Massachusetts jail and noticed that mentally disabled people were being housed with hardened criminals. Her protests and efforts led to the establishment of several institutions and hospitals for the mentally ill.

THE ABOLITIONIST MOVEMENT

Slavery

In the 1830s, the **abolitionist movement** gained momentum. As always, slavery remained a hot topic in the nation. The South found itself dependent on the practice for economic support, while in the North a movement to abolish slavery was growing. White members of this movement were mostly middle-class and educated church people from New England. Black abolitionists were often former slaves. Among key white figures in this movement were William Lloyd Garrison and the Grimke sisters. Garrison founded an influential, anti-slavery newspaper called *The Liberator* in 1831 and helped establish the *American Anti-Slavery*

Society. Meanwhile Sarah and Angelina Grimke were members of a wealthy slaveholding family in South Carolina who became abolitionists and gave anti-slavery speeches.

Important African American abolitionists included David Walker and Frederick Douglass. Born a free black man in Wilmington, North Carolina, Walker witnessed the cruelty of slavery in the South with his own eyes. He eventually made his way to Boston, where he wrote a pamphlet in 1829 entitled, *Appeal to the Colored Citizens of the World*. His efforts and untimely death (most people believe he was murdered) made him an early hero of the movement. Even more famous was Douglass. After escaping slavery in Maryland, he educated himself and became the best known African American speaker for the abolition of slavery.

Frederick Douglass

TEMPERANCE

During the early nineteenth century, the temperance movement began gaining popularity. Members of this movement wanted to limit the use of alcohol. Later, they supported total abstinence (outlawing all alcohol). They eventually succeeded in convincing several states to pass laws prohibiting its sale. Women and Protestant church leaders were very active in the temperance movement. Many US women viewed drinking as an evil that threatened the family. They saw alcohol and saloons as sources of trouble that led men to drink and carouse rather than stay home with their wives and children. Meanwhile, Protestant leaders often saw strong drink as a sin and wanted to pass laws against it.

Temperance Movement

WOMEN'S SUFFRAGE

Elizabeth Cady Stanton

Women who supported abolition and temperance often felt discriminated against by the men in these movements. The offense these women suffered led to the birth of the **women's rights movement**. Women such as **Elizabeth Cady Stanton** helped organize the first women's rights convention in 1848. It was known as the **Seneca Falls Conference**. Between 100 and 300 people attended, including Frederick Douglass. Stanton used the occasion to call for women's suffrage (the right to vote). Although some felt Stanton went too far by demanding suffrage, the conference went a long way in drawing attention to the issue of women's rights.

Other key figures included **Susan B. Anthony** and Julia Ward Howe. Both women were strong supporters of both abolition and women's suffrage. Anthony is best known for her efforts to win women the right to vote. Anthony continued to be a leader of the women's suffrage movement until her death in 1906. Fourteen years after she died, US women won the right to vote nationwide.

Julia Ward Howe was an activist and poet. She is most remembered for writing the words to "The Battle Hymn of the Republic." She was also the first to proclaim Mother's Day and helped edit the magazine, *Woman's Journal*, during the mid 1870s.

Susan B Anthony

Practice 8.2: Religion and Reform

1. The religious movement that sparked a number of reform movements in the 1800s was known as the

    A. First Great Awakening.
    B. Second Great Awakening.
    C. temperance movement.
    D. religious suffrage movement.

2. The movement that called for the end of slavery in the US was the

    A. temperance movement.
    B. suffrage movement.
    C. abolitionist movement.
    D. states' rights movement.

3. Horace Mann was a major figure in

    A. the abolitionist movement.
    B. the Second Great Awakening.
    C. education reform.
    D. prison reform.

4. What was the Seneca Falls Conference, and who were some of the major leaders in the movement it helped promote?

CHAPTER 8 REVIEW

Key Terms, People, and Concepts

Andrew Jackson	Second Great Awakening
Jacksonian Democracy	reform movements
universal suffrage	education reform
spoils system	Horace Mann
laissez-faire economics	prison and mental health reform
strict interpretation	Dorothea Dix
Kitchen Cabinet	abolitionist movement
Indian Removal	temperance movement
Trail of Tears	women's rights movement
South Carolina Nullification Crisis	Elizabeth Cady Stanton
doctrine of nullification	Seneca Falls Conference
states' rights	Susan B. Anthony
two-party system	Julia Ward Howe

Multiple Choice Questions

1. Which of the following statements would President Andrew Jackson have most agreed with?

    A. All people in the United States should be allowed to vote.

    B. Government is too important to be trusted to the decisions of uneducated masses. Only the well-schooled and upper-class should choose the country's leaders.

    C. Any white man has a right to vote.

    D. White people and Native Americans should be allowed to vote because they live free. But not blacks because they are slaves.

2. The practice Jackson introduced of awarding political supporters with government positions was known as the

    A. Kitchen Cabinet.
    C. laissez-faire approach.

    B. spoils system.
    D. doctrine of nullification.

3. A slaveowner in South Carolina would have been most scared of the

    A. Second Great Awakening.
    C. abolitionist movement.

    B. doctrine of nullification.
    D. spoils system.

Democracy, Religion, and Reform

4. Congress passes a law that is very unpopular in certain parts of the country. As a result, the states of Georgia and Tennessee decide not to obey the law because they claim it violates the rights of common farmers. Because the law was properly voted on in Congress and passed, President Andrew Jackson will probably
   A. strike down the law because he is a "common man" president.
   B. insist on Georgia and Tennessee's right to disobey the law.
   C. insist that Georgia and Tennessee obey the law.
   D. have no opinion.

5. Who of the following would have directly benefited from the efforts of Dorothea Dix?
   A. a convicted criminal
   B. a school-aged child
   C. an escaped slave
   D. a woman hoping to vote

6. Susan B. Anthony helped
   A. win women the right to vote.
   B. bring an end to slavery.
   C. limit the sale of alcohol.
   D. begin the Second Great Awakening.

7. Someone who agrees with the ideas of Horace Mann would support which of the following opinions?
   A. Each state has the right to refuse to obey any law it thinks goes against the Constitution.
   B. Prisoners must be rehabilitated; there is no better cause than prison reform.
   C. American democracy and the future of society depends on every child receiving a quality education.
   D. Alcohol is a moral evil; until it is outlawed, the American family is in danger of falling apart.

8. The term "King Andrew" was used to refer to
   A. President Jackson's support of states' rights.
   B. President Jackson's popularity and the fact that nearly every politician wanted to follow him.
   C. Jackson's willingness to follow the decisions of Congress and the Supreme Court.
   D. Jackson's tendency to assume a lot of power when acting as president.

Chapter 9
US History: Secession, Civil War, and Reconstruction

This chapter addresses the following Louisiana iLeap standards:

H-1B-M12	73. Describe the economic, social, and cultural differences between the North and South, including the advantages and disadvantages each had at the outbreak of the Civil War
	74. Explain the impact of the compromises on the issue of slavery and the Dred Scott decision on increasing tensions between the North and South
	75. Explain the immediate and long-term causes of the secession of the southern states and the outbreak of the Civil War
	76. Describe the course of the Civil War, including major turning points and the war's immediate and long-term impact on the North and the South
	77. Explain the purpose, significance, and results of Lincoln's Emancipation Proclamation
	78. Describe provisions of the Thirteenth Amendment and Lincoln's reasons for advancing it, as well as the purpose and significance of the Fourteenth and Fifteenth Amendments
H-1B-M13	79. Describe, compare, and evaluate various reconstruction plans of the post-Civil War South
	80. Explain the growing conflict between Andrew Johnson and Congress and the reasons for and consequences of his impeachment and trial
	81. Describe the successes and failures of Reconstruction, as well as its impact on the South
	82. Explain how the presidential election of 1876 led to the Compromise of 1877 and brought about an end to Reconstruction in the South

9.1 REGIONAL DIFFERENCES

ECONOMIES OF THE NORTH AND SOUTH

During the 1800s, strong regional differences existed between the North and South. The South relied on an **agricultural economy**. Cash crops like cotton provided most of the region's wealth. Dependence on cotton led to the South becoming a **slave society**. The South became reliant on slaves to provide the labor necessary to raise and harvest cotton and other crops. Meanwhile, the North developed a more **industrial economy**. Although northerners relied some on agriculture, they also had more factories and commercial interests. They did not rely on slaves and most northern states outlawed slavery by the mid-1800s.

Slaves on a Southern Plantation

Northern Industry

IMMIGRANTS AND "KNOW-NOTHINGS"

From 1846 to 1854, almost three million **immigrants** arrived in the United States. They immigrated to the US for many reasons. Some wanted to escape wars and political unrest in Europe. Others heard about the land and gold that was available in the western part of the country. A large number of Chinese immigrants played an important role in building western railroads. Many immigrants were Irish Catholics. During the 1840s, a deadly **potato famine** caused mass starvation in Ireland. Rather than go hungry in

Irish Immigrants Arriving in the 1840s

their homeland, large numbers of Irish men and women made their way to the United States in search of a better life. Many settled in large urban areas like New York City. Others made their way west to become farmers or help build railroads.

The American Party

Many white Protestants were not happy about the arrival of immigrants. Some became devoted **nativists**. Nativists opposed immigration. They believed immigrants hurt native-born citizens by taking jobs and "polluting" US culture with foreign traditions and customs. Some nativists joined a secret society called the Order of the Star-Spangled Banner. The organization was so secretive that when members were asked about it, they would only respond, "I know nothing." In 1854, nativists formed their own political party: the **American Party**. People referred to members of the American Party as **Know-Nothings**.

Chapter 9

SLAVERY

As the US acquired new territories in the West, the debate over slavery grew more intense. New territories would eventually become states. States would send representatives and senators to Congress. Therefore, whether or not these territories should allow slavery was the object of much heated discussion among political leaders.

THE MISSOURI COMPROMISE

In 1819, a debate raged in Congress over Missouri's application for statehood. Slave states and free states were equally represented in the Senate. Missouri's admission would disrupt the balance of power. Congress finally agreed on a compromise in 1820. It admitted Missouri as a slave state and Maine as a free state. In addition, the southern boundary of Missouri, 36°30' N latitude, became a dividing

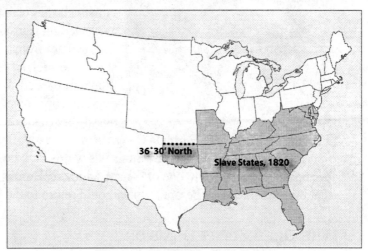

Missouri Compromise Boundaries

line for any new states admitted to the Union. All new states north of the line would be free states, while those to the south would be slave states. The agreement became known as the **Missouri Compromise**. Leaders hoped it would settle the issue of slavery west of the Mississippi River. (Review chapter 2, section 2.2 regarding slavery and the Missouri Compromise.)

THE COMPROMISE OF 1850

Another key piece of legislation was the **Compromise of 1850**. The compromise admitted California to the Union as a free state and declared the unorganized western territories free as well. It also stated that the Utah and New Mexico territories would decide the slavery issue by popular sovereignty. In other words, the people living in these territories would vote on

Bleeding Kansas

whether or not to allow slavery. Attached to the compromise was the Fugitive Slave Law. This law required that northern states return escaped slaves to their owners in the South. Many northern citizens, however, refused to obey it.

THE KANSAS-NEBRASKA ACT

Sumner-Brooks Incident

In 1854, Congress passed the **Kansas-Nebraska Act**. This act allowed the previously free and unorganized territories of Kansas and Nebraska to choose whether or not to permit slavery by popular sovereignty. It repealed the Missouri Compromise and reignited the slavery issue. Both supporters of slavery and abolitionists rushed into Kansas, setting up rival governments. So many violent clashes occurred that the territory became known as "Bleeding Kansas." Meanwhile, in Washington, a fiery senator from Massachusetts named Charles Sumner strongly criticized the act and the senators who wrote it. Sumner opposed slavery. In a speech that spanned two days, he condemned the new law for allowing the possibility of slavery in free territory. A couple of days after the speech, South Carolina Congressman Preston Brooks approached Sumner on the Senate floor. He was insulted by Sumner's words both because he was from the South and because he was related to one of the act's authors. Brooks beat Sumner with a cane so badly that three years passed before Sumner could return to the Senate.

THE DRED SCOTT DECISION

Dred Scott

The 1857 **Dred Scott Case** added to the slavery controversy. Dred Scott was a slave in Missouri. He went with his owner into free territory where he lived for four years. After the owner died, Dred Scott sued for his freedom. The Supreme Court ruled that Scott had no right to sue because, as a slave, he was not a citizen. It also declared that a slave owner could not be deprived of his "property" without due process of law. In other words, under the Fifth Amendment, Scott did not cease to be the owner's property just because they entered free territory. The decision struck down the Missouri Compromise. It also outraged abolitionists and those who favored popular sovereignty because it suggested that slaveholders could keep their slaves in any state, regardless of state law or the will of the people.

THE ABOLITIONIST MOVEMENT

As mentioned in chapter 8, the **abolitionist movement** called for an end to slavery. However, even abolitionists did not always agree. Some wanted **immediate emancipation**. Supporters of this position tended to base their argument on moral grounds. Slavery was evil. Therefore the government should act to immediately outlaw it and free all the slaves at once. Others felt this position was too radical. They feared it would be unwise to release all the slaves immediately without giving states time to adjust economically, socially, and politically. Those who agreed with this position favored **gradual emancipation**. They wanted to reach full emancipation in steps. Most southerners viewed abolitionists as radicals who were out to destroy the southern way of life.

Several key leaders arose out of the abolitionist movement. William Lloyd Garrison was a white abolitionist who printed the anti-slavery newspaper *The Liberator* and helped found the American Anti-slavery Society. Important African American abolitionists included men like **Frederick Douglass** and women like **Harriet Tubman**. After escaping slavery in Maryland, Douglass educated himself and became the most prominent African American speaker for the abolition of slavery. Tubman was an escaped slave who

Abolitionist Rally in the 1800s

returned to the South secretly many times to help other slaves escape by way of the **Underground Railroad**. The Underground Railroad was a series of secret stops along a route that led north to free territory. Tubman, other escaped slaves, freemen (free blacks), and white abolitionists helped many slaves make their way to freedom along the Underground Railroad. (Review chapter 8, section 8.2 regarding the abolitionist movement. Review chapter 1, section 1.2 regarding the Underground Railroad.)

Harriet Tubman

JOHN BROWN'S RAID

John Brown was a white abolitionist and one of the most radical. In October 1859, Brown led a group that attacked the federal arsenal (location where weapons are made and stored) at Harper's Ferry, Virginia. Brown hoped to seize weapons and give them to slaves. He wanted the slaves to rise up in armed rebellion. His plan failed when US troops under the command of Colonel Robert E. Lee surrounded the arsenal and forced Brown's surrender. The government hanged Brown for his actions, but southerners remained concerned. They feared the abolitionist movement more than ever. Southerners believed the South would have to shed blood to protect its way of life.

John Brown

Practice 9.1: Regional Differences

1. Know-Nothings were opposed to
   A. slavery.
   B. abolition.
   C. immigration.
   D. popular sovereignty.

2. The Missouri Compromise was intended to settle the issue of
   A. slavery north of the Ohio River.
   B. popular sovereignty.
   C. slavery west of the Mississippi River.
   D. whether or not Missouri should remain a free state.

3. What was the Supreme Court's ruling in the Dred Scott Case? Why did this ruling upset supporters of popular sovereignty and abolitionists?

4. Describe the difference between immediate and gradual emancipation.

9.2 SECESSION AND CIVIL WAR

THE REPUBLICANS AND THE ELECTION OF 1860

Northern Democrats opposed to slavery, Whigs, and Free Soilers formed a new political party in 1854. (Free Soilers opposed expanding slavery into new territories.) It became known as the **Republican Party**. The Republicans did not call for the immediate abolition of slavery, but they did oppose expanding slavery into new US territories. Within a few years, **Abraham Lincoln** emerged as one of the party's greatest political figures. After

Jefferson Davis   **Abraham Lincoln**

losing a senate race in 1858, Lincoln became the Republican's candidate for president in 1860. The South felt threatened by Lincoln's candidacy because they feared Lincoln would seek to end slavery. They nominated Vice President John Breckinridge. Northern Democrats favored popular sovereignty and nominated Stephen Douglas. When Lincoln won the election, South Carolina responded by seceding from the Union on December 20, 1860. Within two months, six other states had seceded as well: Mississippi, Alabama, Georgia, Florida, Louisiana, and

Texas. In February 1861, southern delegates from the seceded states met in Montgomery, Alabama, where they drafted their own constitution and elected **Jefferson Davis** to serve as president of the new **Confederate States of America.**

FORT SUMTER

President Abraham Lincoln felt he could not let the South secede. However, he also knew that northern citizens did not want war. Many were sick of the slavery debate. They wanted Lincoln to let the South leave the Union and take their disgusting slavery with them. Others wanted to preserve the Union but favored reaching a peaceful solution. Only a few favored force. Even if he wanted to, Lincoln did not have enough support to launch any military action against the Confederacy. If there was going to be a war, the South would have to start it.

Fort Sumter, South Carolina

In April, 1861, Union troops located at **Fort Sumter**, South Carolina, ran low on supplies. Lincoln sent word to the governor of South Carolina that he was sending ships with food for the soldiers but no weapons. South Carolina, however, decided not to allow Union troops to remain any longer. On April 12, Confederate forces opened fire. The South's attack forced the Union troops to leave the fort, but it also gave Lincoln the support he needed for war. Many northerners who originally opposed war now felt the Union had been attacked. They were ready to support their president if he decided military action was necessary. President Lincoln called for 75,000 volunteers. Border states (slave states in the Upper South) were forced to decide whether to support the Union or the Confederacy. Kentucky, Missouri, Maryland, and the northwest region of Virginia remained with the Union. North Carolina, Arkansas, Tennessee, and the rest of Virginia joined the Confederacy. The Confederates then moved their capital from Montgomery, Alabama, to Richmond, Virginia. The **Civil War** had begun.

THE CIVIL WAR

WAR TIME ADVANTAGES

Both sides enjoyed advantages and had to overcome weaknesses during the Civil War. Ultimately, the Union's strengths proved to be too great for the Confederacy.

US History: Secession, Civil War, and Reconstruction

Northern Advantages
The North had more railway lines. They could move troops and supplies faster, to more locations, and in greater numbers.
The Union also had more factories for producing guns, ammunition, uniforms, and so on. In addition, it already had an established government and a standing military force. It did not have to form a government or raise an army.
The Union states were home to two-thirds of the nation's population. Not only did this mean that the Union could send more soldiers into battle, it also supplied the needed labor force to keep the northern economy and production of war supplies going.

Northern Production and Railroads

Southern Advantages
The South did enjoy some advantages, however. For one, the South began the war with better military commanders. General Robert E. Lee was one of the most respected military commanders in history. (He was the same commander who captured John Brown at Harper's Ferry.) Lee was so gifted that President Lincoln actually offered him field command of the Union army at the beginning of the war. Lee turned down the command because he felt loyal to his home state of Virginia. He eventually commanded the Confederate Army of Northern Virginia. Other talented generals, such as Thomas "Stonewall" Jackson, served under Lee in the Confederate army.
Although the South had fewer men, it did not need as many because it intended to fight a defensive war designed to wear down its enemy's will to fight. Much like the colonies during the American Revolution, the Confederacy believed it did not need to win the war; it only needed to resist long enough for the Union to give up.
The South also had greater motivation. Southerners saw themselves as fighting for their homeland and the right to rule themselves. They identified themselves with the founders of the United States who had fought for the same principles against the British. They did not view the conflict as a civil war. Instead, they saw it as a second war for independence.

Southern Landscape

General Robert E Lee

FIRST BULL RUN AND THE ANACONDA PLAN

Bull Run

The **First Battle of Bull Run** (also known as First Manassas because Manassas was the nearest town) was the first confrontation between the two armies. Despite northern advantages, the battle turned out to be a humiliating defeat for the Union. Most northerners expected a short war. After Bull Run, however, it became clear the fighting would go on longer than expected.

Disappointed by his army's defeat, Lincoln adopted General Winfield Scott's **Anaconda Plan**. An anaconda is a large snake that kills its prey by wrapping around it and squeezing it to death. In the same way, Lincoln wanted to cut off Confederate supply lines. The plan would restrict southern trade and communications by seizing control of the Mississippi River. It would also cut Confederate territory in half and put in place coastal blockades (use of naval power to keep ships from entering or leaving enemy ports).

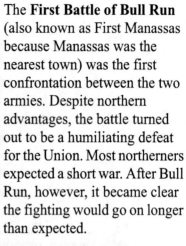
Union Blockade

ANTIETAM

The Battle of Antietam

In 1862, Robert E. Lee took command of the Army of Northern Virginia. One of his first major victories came at the Second Battle of Bull Run (Second Manassas). The battle ended Union hopes of invading Richmond and gave Lee confidence to invade the North.

Lee and his generals tried to maintain secrecy as they planned their invasion. They succeeded until a copy of Lee's orders were found wrapped around some cigars at an abandoned Confederate camp. Now aware of Lee's plans, George McClellan (the Union general) made sure Lee met a prepared Union force at Antietam Creek, Maryland. The battle of **Antietam** proved to be the bloodiest single day of the war. It halted the Confederate army and forced Lee to retreat back into Virginia.

THE EMANCIPATION PROCLAMATION

On January 1, 1863, following a much-needed Union victory at Antietam, President Lincoln issued the **Emancipation Proclamation**. This proclamation freed the slaves in the Confederate States. However, it did nothing to end slavery in slave states loyal to the Union. Lincoln still needed the support of these states and could not risk offending them by forcing them to give up slavery. Still, with this executive order, Lincoln hoped to give the war a moral focus beyond just saving the Union. He also hoped to undermine the South's reliance on slave labor and ensure the support of England and France—both of which had already abolished slavery. The Emancipation Proclamation also encouraged free African Americans to serve in the Union army. Although originally not allowed to enlist, early Union defeats led Congress to authorize accepting African Americans into the army in 1862. On warships, whites and blacks served side by side. In the army, however, African Americans served in all-black regiments under the command of white officers. Seeing their battle as one to free their own people from slavery, African Americans served notably during the war.

Emancipation Proclamation

CHANCELLORSVILLE

The battle of **Chancellorsville** is often called "Lee's perfect battle." Thanks to the efforts of his most gifted general, **Thomas "Stonewall" Jackson**, Lee's army defeated more than 70,000 Union troops with only 40,000 Confederate soldiers. Unfortunately for the Confederacy, Jackson was accidently shot by his own men while scouting the enemy's position at night. His left arm had to be amputated. When Lee heard the news, he responded with his famous quote: "Jackson has lost his left arm, but I have lost my right." Although his injuries were not life threatening, Jackson died after contracting pneumonia during his recovery. As a result, Robert E. Lee was without his most talented and reliable commander for the rest of the war.

Thomas "Stonewall" Jackson

GETTYSBURG

Fought in Pennsylvania, the battle of **Gettysburg** was a key turning point in the war. Without Jackson, Lee's forces proved less aggressive than usual and failed to win valuable high ground early in the battle. Union forces under the command of General George Meade defeated Lee's army and ended any hope the South had of successfully invading the North. With more than 51,000 soldiers killed, wounded, or missing, Gettysburg was the bloodiest battle of the entire Civil War. Four months later, President Lincoln gave his famed Gettysburg Address at a ceremony on the sight of the battlefield. Although a short speech, it stated powerfully Lincoln's desire to see the Union survive and the nation reunited.

Battle at Gettysburg

Soldiers Killed at Gettysburg

VICKSBURG

Ulysses S Grant

In the spring of 1863, the town of Vicksburg, Mississippi, remained the last Confederate obstacle to total Union control of the Mississippi River. Ignoring advice to withdraw, General **Ulysses S. Grant** laid siege to Vicksburg for almost two months. (In a siege, an army surrounds a city, cutting off all supplies. Eventually, inhabitants of the city have to surrender or starve.) By the time the town finally surrendered on July 4, residents were so hungry that they had eaten horses, mules, dogs, and even rats.

Chapter 9

SHERMAN'S ATLANTA CAMPAIGN AND MARCH TO THE SEA

In 1864, Lincoln appointed Grant to be overall commander of the entire Union army. Grant put his most trusted general, **William T. Sherman**, in charge of his western forces. In May, Sherman began an invasion of Georgia. He wanted to reach Atlanta because of its importance as a railway hub. If Sherman took Atlanta, he could hurt the South by disrupting its major rail lines. As Sherman advanced south, General Joseph Johnston's Confederate forces tried to delay his march. Finally, however, Sherman reached Atlanta.

Jefferson Davis was furious with Johnston for letting Sherman reach Atlanta. He replaced Johnston with General John Bell Hood. Hood, however could do no better. His army evacuated Atlanta on September 1, 1864. Sherman's successful **Atlanta Campaign** not only placed the city under Union control, it also increased support for President Lincoln in the North. Before Atlanta, many northerners wanted to replace Lincoln with a president who would negotiate with the South and end the war. After Sherman's success, northerners believed the war could be won and re-elected Lincoln.

Sherman's March to the Sea

William T Sherman

After taking Atlanta, Sherman ordered much of the city burned. He then began a march from Atlanta to Savannah that became known as his **March to the Sea**. On its way to the coast, Sherman's army burned buildings, destroyed rail lines, set fire to factories, and demolished bridges. Sherman hoped to cripple the South's ability to make and ship supplies. Without supplies, the South would have to surrender. People in Savannah were so terrified by news of the destruction that, when Sherman finally reached the city, they surrendered without a fight. Sherman then turned north into the Carolinas. All the while, General Joseph Johnston continued trying to resist Sherman as best he could.

LOUISIANA AND THE CIVIL WAR

New Orleans on the Mississippi River

Many battles took place in Louisiana during the Civil War. The earliest and most important was over **New Orleans** in 1862. New Orleans was the South's major port. It provided the interiors of both the Confederacy and the Union with access to the Gulf of Mexico. It also provided the South with much of its limited industrial production and served as a major finance center. The Confederates were determined to defend New Orleans. But their enemy had more troops, a stronger navy, and better resources. Union attacks forced the Confederates to surrender New Orleans in late April.

The Red River Campaign

Another major event was the **Red River Campaign**. Union forces launched the campaign in 1864 in order to destroy the Confederate army in northern Louisiana. The Union wanted to capture Shreveport and cut off neighboring Texas from the rest of the Confederacy. Texas supplied the South with needed weapons and supplies. Isolating Texas would damage the South's ability to fight. Union General Nathaniel P. Banks planned poorly, however, and the campaign failed to accomplish its goals. It may have actually lengthened the war by wasting resources and men on a failed military effort.

UNION VICTORY

In March 1864, President Lincoln put Ulysses S. Grant in command of the Union army. Grant, knowing he had far more men than Lee, began a campaign designed to crush the Confederate army in a series of head-to-head confrontations. Pushing south, Grant engaged Lee in a number of bloody battles. In less than two months, Grant's army suffered roughly 65,000 casualties. Still, the Union's overwhelming numbers meant that the Confederates were the ones on the retreat. Finally, when the Confederate army found itself surrounded in Virginia, General Lee elected to surrender rather than see more lives lost. On April 9, 1865, Robert E. Lee surrendered to Ulysses S. Grant at **Appomattox Courthouse**. Although some fighting continued afterwards, this effectively ended the war. Two weeks later, the largest and last major surrender of the war took place when General Joseph Johnston surrendered to General William T. Sherman at a farm house in Durham, North Carolina, known as the Bennett Place. The last of Louisiana's troops surrendered just over a month later.

Surrender at Appomattox

Practice 9.2: Secession and Civil War

1. Who was the Republican nominee for president in 1860?

    A. Abraham Lincoln
    B. Stephen Douglas
    C. Jefferson Davis
    D. Robert E. Lee

2. The North enjoyed which of the following advantages during the Civil War?

    A. Northerners were more motivated because they were fighting for their homeland.
    B. Northerners had better generals when the war began.
    C. Northerners had more people and supplies.
    D. Northerners were totally unified in their willingness to fight for the Union as soon as the South seceded.

3. The purpose of the Emancipation Proclamation was to

    A. end slavery in the United States.
    B. hurt the southern war effort.
    C. cut off the South's supplies.
    D. end slavery in states loyal to the Union.

4. Pick one of the battles described in section 9.2 and explain why you feel it was a major battle in the war.

9.3 RECONSTRUCTION

PRESIDENTIAL RECONSTRUCTION

Lincoln Assassination

The Civil War devastated the South. Not only were many of its young men dead, but many of its cities, towns, and plantations were in ruins. Slavery no longer existed, removing the region's major source of labor. After Virginia, South Carolina, and Georgia, Louisiana suffered more than any other state. Before the war, Louisiana ranked as the nation's second wealthiest state and the Confederacy's wealthiest. After the war, it ranked seventeenth nationally and last in the South.

Aware of the South's despair, President Lincoln introduced a plan for rebuilding rather than punishing the southern states. Sadly, he did not live to see the nation healed. On April 14, 1865, just five days after the surrender at Appomattox Courthouse, a Confederate sympathizer named John Wilkes Booth assassinated the president as he attended a play at Ford's Theatre. With Lincoln's death, the presidency fell to **Andrew Johnson**. Johnson was a southerner and one-time slave owner who had remained loyal to the Union. He proved sympathetic to the South. He pursued his own plan of **Presidential Reconstruction**. Under Presidential Reconstruction:

Andrew Johnson

1. Southerners who swore allegiance to the Union were pardoned (forgiven) for seceding and fighting against the United States.

2. Former Confederate states could hold constitutional conventions to set up state governments.

3. States had to cancel secession and ratify the **Thirteenth Amendment** to the Constitution. Unlike the Emancipation Proclamation that only ended slavery in the Confederacy, the Thirteenth Amendment ended slavery throughout the United States.

4. Once the Thirteenth Amendment was ratified, states could hold elections and be part of the Union.

Johnson enacted his brand of reconstruction while Congress was not in session. Under its provisions, many of the same southerners who led the Confederacy held on to their positions of power. Southern states also enacted **black codes**. Although slavery officially ended, southern whites were not about to accept blacks as equals. Black codes were laws that limited the rights of freed blacks so much that they basically still lived as slaves. Blacks had curfews which made it illegal for them to gather after sunset, could be whipped or sold into forced labor if they were convicted of vagrancy (not working), had to agree to work for at least a year for whites, and were often restricted to renting land only in rural areas. Such restrictions allowed whites to continue to control and profit from the labor of African Americans even though slavery did not technically exist.

Black Codes

RADICAL RECONSTRUCTION

When Congress reconvened, conflict quickly arose between Johnson and the **Radical Republicans**. The Radical Republicans were members of the Republican Party who favored a much tougher form of reconstruction. They believed that Johnson's approach did not do enough. They wanted African Americans to have full citizenship rights. They also believed that Congress, not the president, should oversee reconstruction and that the majority of each state's voting population should have to pledge allegiance to the United States before a state could rejoin the Union. The Radical Republicans pushed the Reconstruction Act through Congress in 1867. The law established a much stricter set of guidelines that came to be known as **Radical Reconstruction**. Under Radical Reconstruction:

Radical Republicans

1. The southern states were put under military rule.

2. Southern states had to hold new constitutional conventions.

3. African Americans were allowed to vote.

4. Many southerners who had supported the Confederacy were not allowed to vote (temporarily).

5. Southern states had to guarantee equal rights to African Americans.

6. Southern states had to ratify the **Fourteenth Amendment**. The Fourteenth Amendment made African Americans citizens of the United States and the states in which they lived.

Constitutional Amendments of the Reconstruction Era

Thirteenth Amendment	The Thirteenth Amendment ended slavery throughout the United States.
Fourteenth Amendment	The Fourteenth Amendment proclaims anyone born in the US or naturalized (including freed slaves) to be citizens of the United States and the state in which they live. It also guarantees that no person, regardless of race, may be deprived of life, liberty, or property without due process of law.
Fifteenth Amendment	The Fifteenth Amendment was ratified during the presidency of Ulysses S. Grant. (Grant succeeded Johnson.) It guarantees that no citizen may be denied the right to vote "by the United States or any state on the account of race, color, or previous condition of servitude." It was initially passed to protect African Americans' right to vote.

JOHNSON'S IMPEACHMENT

Thaddeus Stevens

The battle between Congress and President Johnson came to a head in 1868. Johnson tried to fire Secretary of War Edwin Stanton because he was closely tied to the Radical Republicans. However, such a move violated the Tenure in Office Act, which limited the president's power to hire and fire government officials. Led by a fiery Radical Republican named Thaddeus Stevens, Congress voted to **impeach** the president. On May 16, 1868, the Senate voted to spare Johnson's presidency by just one vote. Although his presidency survived, Johnson could not overcome the opposition mounted against him. He agreed not to interfere with Radical Reconstruction, appointed a secretary of war who was devoted to enforcing its provisions, and served only one term as president. The Radical Republicans failed to unseat Johnson, but they succeeded in removing him as an obstacle to their plans.

African Americans and Reconstruction

Sharecropping and Tenant Farming

The Thirteenth Amendment freed the slaves. But African Americans still had to adjust to life after slavery. Although they had their freedom, they had no land or money. In order to survive, many turned to **sharecropping**. Sharecroppers farmed a portion of a white landowner's land in return for housing and a share of the crop. Unfortunately, many sharecroppers fell victim to dishonest landowners who treated them like slaves. Slightly more fortunate African Americans became **tenant farmers**. Tenant farmers paid landowners rent to farm the land and owned the crops they grew. Although tenant farmers were less at the mercy of white landowners than sharecroppers, both lived under systems designed to keep African Americans working white-owned land.

African American Farmer During Reconstruction

The Freedmen's Bureau

In an effort to help freed slaves, Congress created the **Freedmen's Bureau** in 1865. (Freedmen were African Americans freed from slavery.) It was the first federal relief agency in US history. The Freedmen's Bureau provided clothes, medical attention, food, education, and even land to African Americans coming out of slavery. Lacking support, it eventually ended in 1869. However, during its brief time, it helped many slaves transition to freedom throughout the South.

Freedmen's Bureau

EDUCATION AND THE CHURCH

African American Education

The desire for freedom and the need for a sense of community among enslaved African Americans led to the rise of **African American churches**. As one of the few institutions truly owned and controlled by African Americans, black churches became the centers for African American social and political life. Within these churches, African Americans could discuss issues and meet the needs of blacks. As a result, African American ministers became political and social leaders as well as spiritual spepherds.

Blacks also sought **education**. With the help of the Freedmen's Bureau and churches, the African American community established black schools. Teachers were often African American soldiers who had acquired some education in the army. Students included both children and adults.

POLITICS, PRINT, AND SOCIAL DEBATE

Pinckney Pinchback

African Americans played an important role in southern **politics** during Reconstruction. Thanks to Republican policies, some six hundred African Americans served in southern state legislatures, and a few were elected to offices as high as lieutenant-governor. In Louisiana, an African American named Pinckney Pinchback served as the state's second black lieutenant-governor and, for a brief time, as acting governor following a scandal that removed the elected white governor from office. A few blacks also represented southern states in Congress.

Influential **black newspapers** appeared in Louisiana during the war and Reconstruction. The first, *L'Union*, began publication in 1862 and closed operations before the end of the war. The second, the *New Orleans Tribune*, soon followed as the nation's first African American daily publication. By 1867, it was recognized nationally as an official paper. It ceased printing in 1869.

New opportunities presented by Reconstruction also led to conflicts within the black community. Northern blacks and some "elite" southern blacks (usually considered elite because they had been raised free) tended to oppose policies that took land from private landowners and gave it to poorer freedmen. Although they wanted political equality for all blacks, these "elitists" often saw themselves as socially superior to poorer, uneducated blacks who had only recently been emancipated. Meanwhile, southern blacks often resented the northern African Americans who came south and assumed positions that might otherwise have gone to southern blacks.

African American Reading a Newspaper

WHITE RESISTANCE

THE KLU KLUX KLAN AND THE WHITE LEAGUE

Under Radical Reconstruction, black codes lost much of their power. Many southern whites, however, continued to resist giving African Americans equal rights. Some even used violence. Perhaps the most notorious group was the **Ku Klux Klan**. A secretive organization whose members dressed in hooded white robes, the Klan used threats, violence, and murder to intimidate blacks and those who helped them. The Klan often practiced lynchings (mob-initiated killings in which the victim is kidnapped and murdered).

Ku Klux Klan Members

In Louisiana, the Knights of the White Camellia used tactics similar to the Ku Klux Klan. They later gave way to an even more notorious group known as the **White League**. The White League used violence to keep African Americans and Republicans from voting. Their actions resulted in the murders of several public officials and contributed to a number of bloody riots.

The White League

CARPETBAGGERS AND SCALAWAGS

Cartoon Depicting a Carpetbagger

As Reconstruction continued, many in the South continued to grow bitter towards the Union and those who profited from Reconstruction. Southerners especially resented **carpetbaggers**. These were northerners who came to the South to do business. Many of them were former Union officers, but others were teachers, ministers, lawyers, and so forth. They were called "carpetbaggers" because it was said that they had "stuffed some clothes into a carpet bag" and rushed south to get rich. Southerners believed carpetbaggers took advantage of southern suffering to make money.

Most white southerners also hated **scalawags**. Scalawags were southern Republicans who supported Reconstruction. Southern newspapers often published their names to make sure that they suffered persecution at the hands of southern citizens and groups like the Ku Klux Klan and the White League. On more than one occasion, hatred of scalawags led to the establishment of dual governments in Louisiana. While Republicans fought to maintain control, Democrats that opposed Reconstruction claimed to have won local elections. A number of violent battles broke out, leading to many deaths. The Republicans managed to cling to power until 1876, when a Democratic administration once again claimed to be the rightful government of Louisiana. This time, national events enabled the Democrats to remain in power and push blacks and southern Republicans out of the government.

Sam Tilden

THE COMPROMISE OF 1877

Rutherford B Hayes

In 1869, Civil War hero and Republican candidate Ulysses S. Grant replaced Andrew Johnson as president. He served two terms. However, because of the bad economy when he left office and the many scandals during his presidency, the Democrats felt that they could win the White House in 1876. They nominated New York's Governor Samuel Tilden. The Republicans nominated Ohio's Governor Rutherford B. Hayes. Tilden received more popular votes than Hayes, but Republicans disputed the results in some states. When the two parties could not agree on the legitimate outcome, Congress appointed a commission to settle the controversy. The result was an agreement that became known as the **Compromise of 1877**. The Democrats agreed to Hayes being president in return for the Republicans agreeing to end Reconstruction. Southern states received federal money, more power to govern themselves, and a promise from the national government to withdraw federal troops. The decision brought Reconstruction to an end and began the era of the "Solid South." The term refers to the fact that, for nearly a century after Reconstruction, Southerners remained distrustful of the Republican Party and *solidly* supported Democratic candidates. As white southerners seized more control over their own state governments, African Americans lost many of the rights and positions of influence they had gained under Reconstruction.

Practice 9.3: Reconstruction

1. Which of the following was a major difference between Presidential Reconstruction and Radical Reconstruction?

   A. Presidential Reconstruction sought to punish the South, but Radical Reconstruction wanted to rebuild the South.

   B. Abraham Lincoln proposed Presidential Reconstruction, while Andrew Johnson proposed Radical Reconstruction.

   C. Presidential Reconstruction wanted to continue slavery, but Radical Reconstruction was designed to end slavery.

   D. Presidential Reconstruction was more lenient towards the South, while Radical Reconstruction imposed harsher conditions.

2. After the Civil War, the South could best be described as

   A. strong because it was once again part of the Union.

   B. devastated economically, politically, and socially.

   C. reconstructed because President Lincoln introduced measures to help the southern states.

   D. fortunate because the war ended before most states' economies were affected.

3. Which of the following ended slavery in the United States?

   A. Emancipation Proclamation   C. Radical Reconstruction

   B. Thirteenth Amendment   D. Fourteenth Amendment

4. Describe some of the ways Radical Reconstruction affected southern African Americans.

5. Describe the circumstances that led to the Compromise of 1877. What effect did the compromise have on the South?

Chapter 9 Review

Key Terms, People, and Concepts

agricultural economy
slave society
industrial economy
immigrants
potato famine
nativists
American Party
Know-Nothings
Missouri Compromise
Compromise of 1850
Kansas-Nebraska Act
Dred Scott Case
abolitionist movement
immediate emancipation
gradual emancipation
William Lloyd Garrison
Frederick Douglass
Harriet Tubman
Underground Railroad
John Brown's Raid
Republican Party
Abraham Lincoln
Jefferson Davis
Confederate States of America
Fort Sumter
Civil War

northern advantages
southern advantages
First Battle of Bull Run

Anaconda Plan
Antietam
Emancipation Proclamation
Chancellorsville
Thomas "Stonewall" Jackson
Gettysburg
Ulysses S. Grant
William T. Sherman
Atlanta Campaign
March to the Sea
New Orleans
Red River Campaign
Appomattox Courthouse
Andrew Johnson
Presidential Reconstruction
Thirteenth Amendment
black codes
Radical Republicans
Radical Reconstruction
Fourteenth Amendment
Fifteenth Amendment
Johnson's impeachment
sharecropping
tenant farming
Freedmen's Bureau
African American churches, education, newspapers, and politics
Ku Klux Klan
White League
carpetbaggers and scalawags

Chapter 9

Multiple Choice Questions

1. Members of the American Party were **most** afraid of
   A. Reconstruction.
   B. Lincoln's slavery policies.
   C. foreign cultural influences.
   D. African Americans gaining political power.

2. Both abolitionists and supporters of popular sovereignty were upset about the
   A. Kansas-Nebraska Act.
   B. Dred Scott decision.
   C. Compromise of 1850.
   D. Missouri Compromise.

Look at the map below and answer the following question.

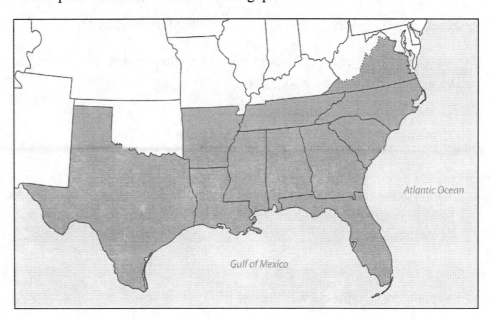

3. The map depicts
   A. free states prior to the civil war.
   B. states that became part of the Union as part of the Compromise of 1850.
   C. states that remained loyal to the Union after the Confederacy seceded.
   D. states where slaves were declared free under the Emancipation Proclamation.

Read the list below and answer the following question.
- famines
- political unrest
- wars

4. Which of the following would be the **best** heading for the list above?
   A. Reasons the South Seceded
   B. Causes of the Civil War
   C. Factors That Led to Immigration
   D. Issues That Helped Lincoln Win the Presidency.

5. An escaped slave who made his way to freedom by way of the Underground Railroad would likely be most indebted to
   A. John Brown.
   B. Abraham Lincoln.
   C. Jefferson Davis.
   D. Harriet Tubman.

6. More railways, larger population, and more industry were all advantages enjoyed by
   A. the Union during the Civil War.
   B. the Confederacy during the Civil War.
   C. immigrants who came to the US during the mid-1800s.
   D. the state of Louisiana as the Civil War ended.

7. Which of the following was the bloodiest battle of the Civil War and ended Robert E. Lee's hopes of successfully invading the North?
   A. Antietam
   B. Chancellorsville
   C. Gettysburg
   D. Vicksburg

8. Appomatox Courthouse was the site of
   A. Lincoln's second inauguration.
   B. Lee's surrender to Grant.
   C. the Freedmen's Bureau.
   D. the meeting that led to the Compromise of 1877.

9. A white, southern Democrat in 1877 would have been **most** supportive of
   A. Radical Reconstruction.
   B. the Thirteenth, Fourteenth, and Fifteenth Amendments.
   C. laws protecting carpetbaggers and scalawags.
   D. the compromise that made Rutherford B. Hayes president.

iLeap 7th Grade Social Studies Practice Test 1

The purpose of this practice test is to measure your progress in United States Social Studies. This test is based on the Louisiana iLeap Seventh Grade test in Social Studies and adheres to the sample question format provided by the Louisiana Department of Education.

General Directions:

1. Read all directions carefully.

2. Read each question or sample. Then choose the best answer.

3. Choose only one answer for each question. If you change an answer, be sure to erase your original answer completely.

Results of the Electoral Vote for 1944, 1964, and 1984

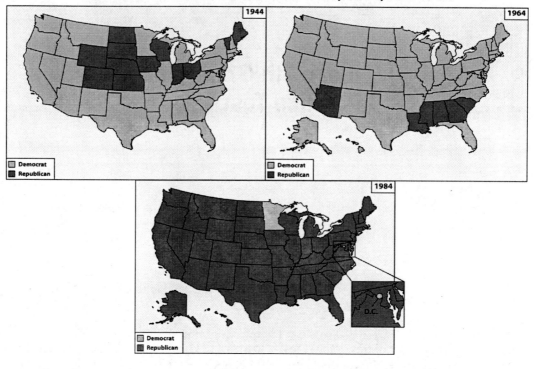

1. Based on the maps above, which statement is **most definitely** true?

   A Democrats have won every presidential race since 1944

   B Republicans have won every presidential race but one since 1944

   C Republicans cannot win in states the once belonged to the Confederacy

   D The "Solid South" no longer exists

2. Which of the following **best** describes a republic?

   A Every citizen has the right to vote on important issues.

   B A king or queen has absolute rule.

   C A king or queen shares power with a legislature.

   D Citizens elect representatives to make decisions on their behalf.

3. South Carolina seceded from the Union on December 20, 1860. What later event was **most** influenced by this decision?

   A Dred Scott case

   B Thomas Jefferson's agreement to the Louisiana Purchase

   C establishment of the Confederate States of America

   D Franklin Pierce's decision to pay for the Gadsden Purchase

4 Which of the following statements **best** describes how the United States acquired much of its southwest territory from Mexico?

A Mexico had no use for the land and was happy to sell it.

B The US defeated Mexico in a war and the Mexicans were in no position to resist.

C Mexico had allied with the Confederacy and had to give up the land as part of the surrender that ended the Civil War.

D Mexico gave it as a gift to establish friendly relations with the United States.

> "We hold these truths to be self-evident, that all men are created equal, that they are endowed by their Creator with certain unalienable Rights, that among these are Life, Liberty and the Pursuit of Happiness. That to secure these rights, Governments are instituted among Men, deriving their just powers from the consent of the governed, That whenever any Form of Government becomes destructive to these ends, it is the Right of the People to alter or abolish it…"
>
> The Declaration of Independence 1776

5 According to the passage above, which of the following statements is the **most** accurate?

A The Founding Fathers of the United States believed the main role of government is to maintain law and order.

B The Second Continental Congress wanted a government that would serve the will of the people.

C The Articles of Confederation failed to provide a strong enough defense.

D Governments are obligated to prevent and resist rebellions against their authority.

6 The War of 1812 was an example of which of the following?

A how war has historically been used to resolve social conflicts

B the power of compromise to settle disputes

C the determination of Andrew Jackson to drive the Spanish out of Florida

D the alliance that formed between the United States and Great Britain after the American Revolution

7 Coming to the United States to find work, political freedom, and better opportunities can all be **best** described as what?

A economic reasons for immigration

B political reasons for immigration

C pull factors for immigration

D push factors for immigration

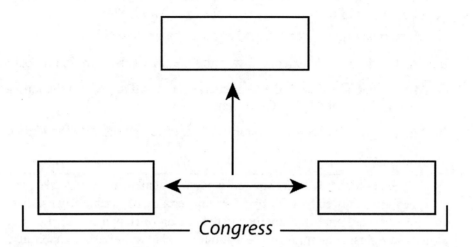

8 Look at the diagram above depicting how a bill becomes law. Which of the following bodies of government should **not** be included in the diagram?

C-1A-M7

    A Supreme Court   **C** House of Representatives

    B president of the United States   **D** US Senate

9 Which of the following effects did urbanization have on the US?

G-1C-M3

    A. The number of immigrants decreased.   C. Nativism ceased to exist.

    B. Ethnic diversity increased.   D. Industrialization slowed down.

Use this list to answer question 10.

- wars and political unrest in Europe
- land and gold rush of the West
- potato famine in Ireland
- railroad workers needed

10 Which of the following is the **best** heading for the list?

H-1B-M10

    A Contributions to the rise of Slavery in the South

    B Causes of Immigration to the US between 1846 – 1854

    C Effects of Jackson's Indian Removal Policy

    D Causes of the War of 1812

11 Miriam is an elected representative from Louisiana. She represents a specific district and serves in the federal government. If Miriam wants to keep her seat, she will have to run for re-election every two years. Miriam is part of which branch of government?

    A executive   **B** legislative   **C** judicial   **D** state

Use this quotation to answer question 12.

> "We should be allowed to make our own laws. It is our right to decide whether slavery is permitted in our state. The federal interference in the issue over slavery is unjust and a violation of states' rights."

12 This quotation reflects a point of view towards slavery during the nineteenth century. Who is **most likely** responsible for this quote?

    A. British General   C. African American soldier

    B. Native American   D. southern political leader

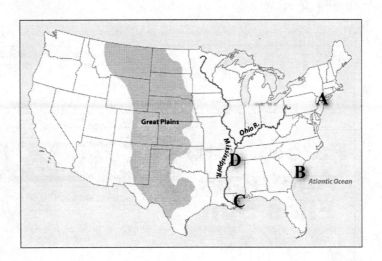

13 Look at the map above. What would you **most likely** find in the areas labeled **A** and **D** during the mid-1800s?

    A Native American reservations.

    B gold mines.

    C cities.

    D cattle ranches.

Practice Test 1

14 How did the South's defeat in the Civil War **most** affect US political culture?

   A The Bill of Rights did not apply to southerners for almost one hundred years after the war.

   B Democrats replaced Republicans as the ruling party in the South soon after the war.

   C It increased the power of the federal government over the states.

   D It ended the political struggles of African Americans.

15 The federal government is made up of a legislative branch that makes laws, an executive branch that enforces laws, and a judicial branch that rules on the constitutionality of the laws. Such a system is an example of what?

   A checks and balances that ensure federalism

   B separation of powers meant to limit government

   C the doctrine of nullification's influence on the Constitution

   D concurrent powers

16 Based on the newspaper article above, Mr. Sandar will **most likely** claim that which of his constitutional rights has been violated?

   A freedom of religion   **C** due process

   B freedom of speech   **D** protection against unlawful search and seizure

17 Passing laws, impeaching public officials, approving executive appointments, and minting money are all powers of which body of government?

    A Congress   **C** Supreme Court

    B president   **D** Freedmen's Bureau

18 Which of the following is **not** a role of political parties?

    A nominate candidates for public office

    B engage in diplomacy with foreign nations

    C help limit the voting choice

    D support political platforms

- Sanctions
- Diplomacy
- Embargo
- Military Action

19 The list above mentions several ways the US chooses to interact with foreign countries. Which one would a president **most likely** use last?

    A diplomacy   **C** military action'

    B embargoes   **D** sanctions

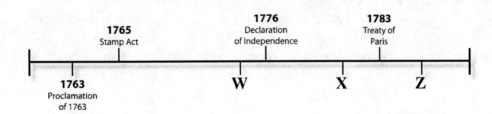

20 On the timeline above, which of the following events should be inserted at the point labeled X?

    A Battle of Yorktown

    B Constitutional Convention

    C Gettysburg

    D the Boston Tea Party

21 What kind of areas were western settlers **most likely** to migrate to during the 1800s?
   A land far from rivers and oceans
   C territories experiencing famines
   B regions with available land or gold
   D areas full of wars and unrest

22 Which of the following was **not** a US export that contributed to US interdependence with Europe and other parts of the world during the eighteenth and nineteenth centuries?
   A cotton   B tobacco   C books   D timber

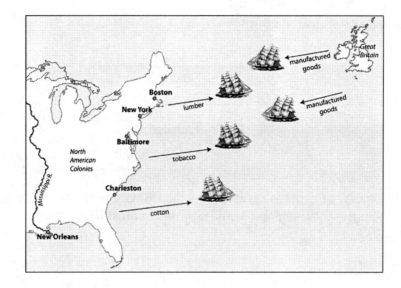

23 The picture above **best** illustrates which of the following?
   A secession   B mercantilism   C independence   D revolution

24 The president appoints people to serve as federal judges. However, before they can take the bench, the US Senate must first approve their appointments. What principle of government is this an example of?
   A federalism
   C checks and balances
   B democracy
   D due process

25 Debating and passing new laws, peacefully replacing leaders through elections, and ratifying amendments to the Constitution are all examples of which of the following?
   A strict interpretations of the Constitution
   B the doctrine of nullification
   C methods of political change
   D acts of secession

A	B
"Each state retains its sovereignty, freedom, and independence…"	"We the people of the United States, in order to form a more perfect union…"
one legislative vote per state in the national government	two houses comprise Congress, with each state represented by population in one house and entitled to two senators in the other
national government may not impose taxes	national government may impose taxes

26 What are lists A and B above **most likely** contrasting?

   A the Declaration of Independence and the US Constitution

   B the Articles of Confederation and the US Constitution

   C the Emancipation Proclamation and the Thirteenth Amendment

   D Presidential Reconstruction and Radical Reconstruction

27 Jordan serves on the president's cabinet. She is responsible for foreign relations. She oversees ambassadors and often represents the president in meetings with foreign leaders. Jordan is **most likely** what?

   A vice president

   B speaker of the House

   C president pro tempore

   D secretary of state

28 Which of the following did President George Washington issue in an attempt to protect the new government?

   A Proclamation of Neutrality

   B Intolerable acts

   C Sons of Liberty

   D Proclamation of 1763

Use this quotation to answer question 29.

> "I decided to follow the example of Sam Adams and encourage all my friends to protest by boycotting the English goods and joining the Sons of Liberty. I was there that night. It was our intent to throw it overboard because they would not remove it from our harbor."

29 Which event was the person who made this statement **most likely** referring to?

   A The Boston Massacre

   B The Boston Tea Party

   C Lexington and Concord

   D the attack on Fort Sumter

30 Boris wants to become a US citizen. Neither he nor his parents were born in the US, but he has lived in the country legally for nine years. He is a respected member of his community, speaks English, and has never broken the law. In order to become a citizen, Boris will have to do which of the following?

A leave the country and re-enter

B take the remaining steps to be naturalized

C nothing, because after five years in the country one becomes a citizen automatically

D He cannot become a citizen because neither he nor his parents were born in the US.

Use the maps below to answer question 31.

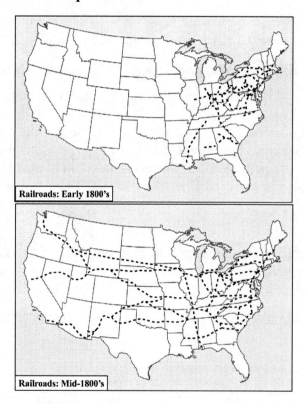

31 Based on the information depicted in the map above, which of the following was **most likely** true?

A More buffalo roamed the Great Plains in 1860 than did in 1810.

B More white settlers moved west in 1860 than did in 1810.

C The number of immigrants to the United States decreased during the 1800s.

D Native Americans relied heavily on railroads during the mid-1800s.

- The Monroe Doctrine
- War of 1812
- War on Terror
- Sanctions against North Korea

32 Which of the following is the **best** heading for the list above?
   A Sectionalism in the United States
   B Events That Led to Manifest Destiny
   C Historical Examples of Successful Diplomacy
   D US Attempts to Address Foreign Policy Issues

33 Which was a **main** purpose of Hamilton's Economic Plan?
   A pay off the national debt incurred during the American Revolution
   B make cotton the basis of southern economy
   C create a large army to protect the US from European invasions
   D improve relations with Native Americans

> "I firmly believe that certain matters should be decided by the states and not the federal government. We need less national government, not more. That is the way the Founding Fathers intended it. I certainly don't support a modern-day 'doctrine of nullification,' but I do believe we must return more power back to the states."
>
> – Republican presidential candidate 2008

34 The politician who made the quote above was in favor of what principle?
   A federalism   C confederation
   B mercantilism   D checks and balances

35 Paul wants to run for national public office. He is 33 years old, was born in the United States, and has never committed any crime. Which of the following offices is Paul eligible to run for?
   A president   C vice president
   B a seat in Congress   D all of the above

36 Loyalists are **best** described as
   A colonists who opposed Great Britain's policies
   B colonists who opposed immigration
   C colonists who wanted to remain part of Great Britain
   D colonists who refused to pay taxes

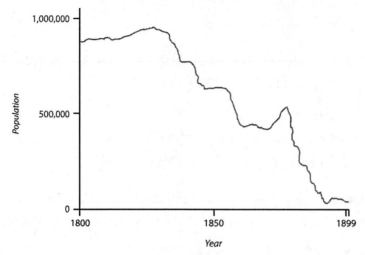

37. Which of the following is the **most likely** explanation for the data shown in the graph above?

   A Manifest Destiny

   B wars launched by Native Americans.

   C the weaknesses in the Articles of Confederation.

   D the Civil War

38. Which of the following did **not** contribute to the call for a new constitution in 1787?

   A the need for a national defense
   C disunity among different regions

   B economic troubles
   D failure to protect states' rights

39. Which of the following **best** describes economic reasons for the American Revolution?

   A Great Britain felt that colonial taxes were too high.

   B Colonists resented British restrictions on trade.

   C Great Britain repealed the Stamp Act.

   D Colonists were upset about British boycotts of colonial products.

40. Which of the following contributed **most** to the end of Reconstruction in the South?

   A. Compromise of 1877
   C. Dred Scott Case

   B. Kansas-Nebraska Act
   D. The White League

iLeap 7th Grade Social Studies Practice Test 2

The purpose of this practice test is to measure your progress in United States Social Studies. This test is based on the Louisiana iLeap Seventh Grade test CRCT in Social Studies and adheres to the sample question format provided by the Louisiana Department of Education.

General Directions:

1. Read all directions carefully.

2. Read each question or sample. Then choose the best answer.

3. Choose only one answer for each question. If you change an answer, be sure to erase your original answer completely.

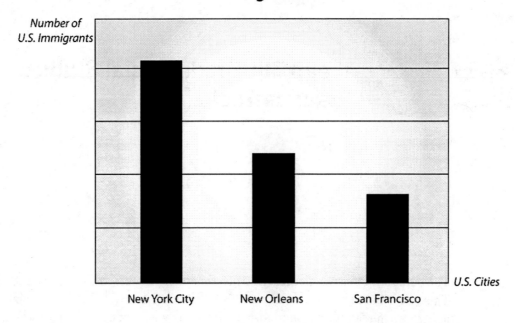

1. According to the graph above, which of the following was **most likely** common in New York City in 1850?

   A Manifest Destiny
   B secessiion
   C nativism
   D reconstruction

2. When the United States government was first formed, it was intended to ensure that power would remain in the hands of an "elite" ruling class that would elect leaders and make decisions on behalf of the people. Such a government is called what?

   A democracy   B monarchy   C republic   D theocracy

3. The Missouri Compromise was intended to settle the issue of slavery west of the Mississippi River. If the compromise had ended all slavery instead, what effect could this have had on the history of the US?

   A The United States would not be as economically stable.
   B The Boston Tea Party wouldn't have happened.
   C The Civil War may never have occurred.
   D The Gold Rush of California would have ended sooner.

> "We the people of the United States, in order to form a more perfect union, establish justice, insure domestic tranquility, provide for the common defense, promote the general welfare, and secure the blessings of liberty to ourselves and our posterity, do ordain and establish this Constitution for the United States of America."
>
> Preamble to the United States Constitution 1787

4 According to the Preamble, which of the following statements is **most** accurate?

   A The national government should give more power to the states.

   B Framers of the Constitution wanted to promote sectionalism.

   C The original purpose of the Constitution was to declare independence.

   D The role of government should be to ensure continued freedom.

5 The discovery of gold in the Rocky Mountains and California had which of the following effects?

   A Settlers were drawn to these regions because they hoped to get rich.

   B White settlers abandoned these regions because they feared mining would upset their daily lives.

   C Environmentalists and miners left these regions.

   D Settlers trickled into these regions very slowly because the regions were hard to get to.

6 Slavery, Reconstruction, and the structure of US government under the Constitution were all issues that were greatly affected by which of the following?

   A Manifest Destiny   **C** political compromises

   B the Emancipation Proclamation   **D** federalism

7 Which **best** describes the effects of the Civil War on the South?

   A The South's victory allowed it to flourish economically.

   B African Americans were instantly treated as equals to whites.

   C The economy was devastated.

   D The economy immediately changed from agricultural to industrial.

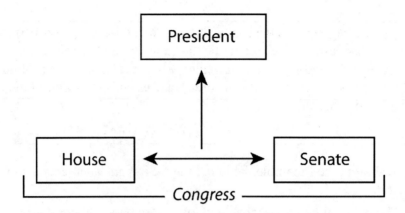

8 Look at the diagram above depicting how a bill becomes law. Where would you draw the arrow if you wanted to show what happens when a **veto** occurs?   C-1A-M7

  A from the House to the president

  B from Congress to the president

  C from the Senate to the president

  D from the president back to Congress

9 Immigration and industrialization helped lead directly to which of the following?   G-1C-M3

  A federalism   C urban growth

  B the "Solid South"   D the Three-fifths Compromise

10 Thomas is an elected representative from Tennessee. He represents a specific district and serves in the federal government. He runs for re-election every two years and hopes to one day be speaker. In what body of government does Thomas serve?   C-1A-M6

  A presidential cabinet   C House of Representatives

  B United States Senate   D Supreme Court

11 Which of the following is an example of foreign policy issues facing the United States during the 1800s?   C-1C-M3

  A Conflicts between Federalists and Anti-federalists over the correct interpretation of the Constitution.

  B the War with Mexico

  C the South Carolina Nullification Crisis

  D the American Revolution

Use these lists to answer question 12.

A	B
Sons of Liberty	Proclamation of 1763
Committees of Correspondence	Stamp Act
Patriots	Intolerable Acts
Boston Tea Party	Tea Act

12. What are lists **A** and **B most likely** addressing?

   A conflicts between the thirteen American colonies and Great Britain

   B tensions between Native Americans and Chinese immigrants

   C Presidential and Radical Reconstruction

   D Hamilton's economic plan and the Proclamation of Neutrality

13. In 1868, Congress claimed that President Andrew Johnson was guilty of wrongdoing and tried to remove him from office. What is such action called?

   A due process

   B legislative process

   C impeachment

   D recall

14. Which of the following statements **best** describes the affects of the Second Great Awakening?

   A led to involvement in social causes and inspired several reform movements

   B led to a policy of rewarding political supporters and the creation of the spoils system

   C led to the Indian Removal Act and an attempt to relocate Native Americans to reservations

   D led to Jacksonian democracy and the belief that women should be allowed to vote

15. The Mexican-American War ended in 1848 and led to

   A the Monroe Doctrine and more freedom for the US.

   B the Louisiana Purchase and a stronger US army.

   C the Gadsden Purchase and more land for the US.

   D fewer supporters of Manifest Destiny.

Use this quotation to answer question 16.

> "These foolish colonists treat the Act as a game. Then they dare to protest that they're not respected. You cannot lie, cheat, and smuggle and expect to be treated cordially by the mother country! Our writs of assistance give us the authority to board any ship we choose. I'm only doing my job to ensure that the crown collects the money it deserves."

16 This quotation was taken from an article in 1773. With which statement would the author of the article **most likely** agree?

   A The Boston Tea Party was not justified.

   B The Boston Tea Party was necessary.

   C Great Britain had no right to tax imported goods.

   D Colonists were respectful of the British government.

17 Which of these statements was a policy of Jacksonian Democracy?

   A Native Americans should be allowed to vote.

   B Only elites and upper class men should be allowed to vote.

   C All white men should be free to vote.

   D Only white males who owned property should be allowed to vote.

18 Which of the following did **not** involve the Atlantic Ocean?

   A immigration during the 1800s

   B Manifest Destiny

   C mercantilism

   D George Washington's victory at Yorktown

19 The Missouri Compromise was intended to accomplish what?

   A end the Civil War

   B justify the Emancipation Proclamation

   C open the Northwest Territory to exploration

   D settle the issue of slavery in new territories

20 The economic relationship between Great Britain and the North American colonies can **best** be described how?

   A unimportant   C interdependent

   B barely noticeable   D hard to understand

Use the graph below to answer question 9.

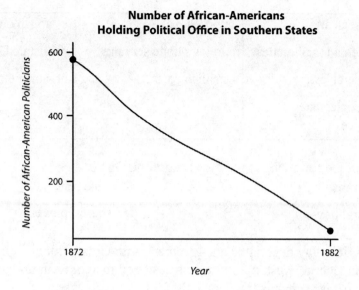

21 Which of the following events **best** explains the trend depicted in the graph above?

A the start of the Civil War

B the Emancipation Proclamation

C Compromise of 1877

D failure of the Articles of Confederation

> "What God tried to do by way of famine, now we, as Christian Americans, must do. And by Christian I mean true Christians—not like them Catholic heathens. And by American, I mean true Americans—born and bred here; not arrived like some ship rat. Blast 'em I say. Blast 'em all the way back to the island from which they come!"
>
> – Nativist speech 1850

22 The above speech is **most likely** attacking which of the following?

A the Confederacy

B Chinese immigrants

C Native Americans

D Irish immigrants

23 When do members of political parties choose their candidates for a particular office?

A during a primary election

B in the general election

C during a constitutional convention

D at a party platform session

A	B	C
maintain an army	impose taxes	establish cities/towns
sign international treaties	employ public servants	pass state laws
pass federal laws	establish courts	organize elections
regulate interstate commerce		

24. Which of the following is the **best** heading for list **B**?
   A federalism
   B federal powers
   C state powers
   D shared powers

25. In 1794, John Jay negotiated an agreement with Great Britain on behalf of President George Washington. It was designed to avoid war and improve trade. What is such an agreement called?
   A diplomacy   B a treaty   C an embargo   D a tariff

26. The Stamp Act was established in 1765. One colonial leader angrily responded, "No taxation without representation!" Whose point of view does this statement **most likely** reflect?
   A northern Patriot
   B southern Loyalist
   C nativist
   D African American slave

Use the timeline below to answer question 27.

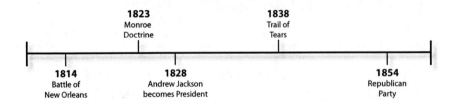

27. On the timeline above, which of the following should be inserted after "Andrew Jackson becomes President"?

   A War of 1812

   B end of the Federalist Party

   C the Cherokee settle in the western Carolinas

   D spoils system

28 Which of the following is **not** an unalienable right according to the Declaration of Independence?

A life

B money

C liberty

D the pursuit of happiness

> "In the midst of great debate over how each state would be represented, Connecticut's Roger Sherman finally presented a plan that won approval. The legislature would consist of two houses. In one house, each state would be awarded a number of representatives based on population. This satisfied the large states. The second house would consist of senators, two per state, to be elected by state legislatures. This reassured the smaller states..."

29 Which of the following is the text book excerpt above **most likely** referring to?

A the Missouri Compromise

B the South Carolina Nullification Crisis

C the Great Compromise

D the Monroe Doctrine

30 Which of the following **best** describes the role of an ambassador?

A to decide US foreign policy towards a certain nation

B. make decisions about embargoes

C. represent the president in a foreign nation

D. represent Congress during summits

31 In order for the Sixth and Seventh amendments to be effective, US citizens must be willing to do which of the following?

A serve on juries

B protect due process

C exercise free speech

D respect states' rights

32 Which of the following groups made their way to Louisiana in the late 1750s?

A Irish survivors of the potato famine

B Chinese railroad workers

C Acadians

D Know-Nothings

Use the graph below to answer question 33.

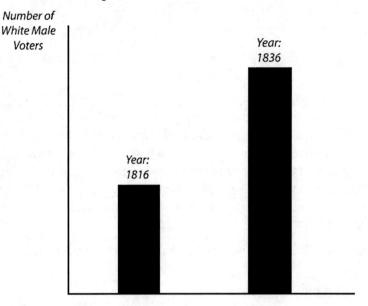

33. Which of the following **most likely** explains the difference in height of the two bars on the graph above?

   A Andrew Jackson's support for universal suffrage

   B the Louisiana Purchase

   C the Civil War

   D Abraham Lincoln's opposition to slavery

34. The failure of the Articles of Confederation helped demonstrate which of the following?

   A Citizens must be willing to pay taxes if they want an effective national government.

   B The United States was not ready for independence and needed to be ruled by Great Britain a while longer.

   C It is safer to give more power to state governments than it is to give power to a national government.

   D A loose interpretation of the Constitution is better than a strict interpretation.

35 Jonathon, a white male living in the nineteenth century, believes it is the United States' destiny to spread democracy west to the Pacific Ocean. Jonathon represents which ideology?

A Second Great Awakening

B Manifest Destiny

C American System

D Sectionalism

Use this passage to answer question 36.

> "He was chosen to lead the Continental Army during the Revolutionary War. He was a great leader and won key battles. He later presided over the Constitutional Convention and became a President of the United States."

36 Which figure in the American Revolution is this passage referring to?

A Benjamin Franklin

B Thomas Jefferson

C John Adams

D George Washington

37 During the Civil War, President Abraham Lincoln had many people arrested and held in jail for long periods without standing trial. He did this because he feared their criticisms of the war would help destroy the Union. Lincoln's actions demonstrate which of the following?

A grounds for impeachment

B the doctrine of nullification

C conflict between civil liberties and national security

D the ineffectiveness of the Constitution

38 Jury duty, obeying laws, paying taxes, and serving in public office are all examples of what?

A freedoms guaranteed by the Bill of Rights

B responsibilities of US citizenship

C keys to due process

D amendments added to the Constitution

Use the map below to answer question 36.

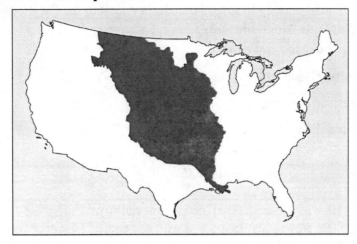

39 Which US president is credited with purchasing the territory on the map above?

    A George Washington

    B Thomas Jefferson

    C James Monroe

    D James K. Polk

> "It has continually played an important role in US history. Before the Louisiana Purchase, it served as a natural border between the US and western territories. After 1803, it served to divide the nation in two between, east and west. Its importance in terms of trade and transportation made cities like New Orleans targets of invasion during the War of 1812 and later, the American Civil War..."

40 The magazine article above is referring to the

    A Ohio River Valley.

    B Gadsden Purchase.

    C Oregon Trail.

    D Mississippi River.

Numerics
49ers 34, 131

A
abolitionist movement 152, 160
Acadians 41
activism
   boycotts 84
   marches 84
   political 83
   rallies 84
   strikes 84
Adams, John 74, 107, 116, 117
Adams, John Quincy 127, 146
Adams, Samuel 107
Adams-Onis Treaty 127
African American
   church 176
   education 176
   in the Northwest Territory 30
   in the War 167
   limited rights 173
   politics 176
   postwar South 177
   Reconstruction 175
   religion 176
   transition to freedom 175
aid
   economic 87
Alien Act 117
Allen, Ethan 111
alternatives 101
ambassador 89, 91
Amendment
   17 59
   Eighth 77
   Fifth 76
   First 75
   Fourth 76
   Ninth 77
   Second 76
   Seventh 76
   Sixth 76
   Tenth 77
   Third 76
   Thirteenth 172, 175
amendment 85
amendment process 84
American Anti-Slavery Society 152
American Party 158
   Know-Nothings 158
American Revolution 30, 48, 78, 97, 106, 109, 151
   key figures 106
American System 133
Anaconda Plan 166
Anthony, Susan B 154
Antietam 167
Appalachian Mountains 28
appellate 64
Appomattox Courthouse 171, 172
archives 100
Arnold
   Benedict 110
Articles of Confederation 72
Atlanta campaign 169

B
Battle of Bunker Hill 110
Battle of Gettysburg 168
Battle of Guilford Courthouse 112
Battle of New Orleans 125
Bennett Place 171
Bessemer process 136
bill 59, 66
   constitutional process 66
Bill of Rights 74, 75, 84
   citizen rights and responsibilities 85
black codes 173, 177
Bleeding Kansas 160
Boone, Daniel 28
Booth, John Wilkes 172
Boston Massacre 105
Boston Tea Party 30, 105
boycott 104
Breckinridge, John 162
Brooks, Preston 160
Brown, John 161
Burr, Aaron
   duel with Hamilton 117

C
Cajuns 41
Calhoun, John C 149
California Gold Rush 34, 40, 131
candidates 82
carpetbagger 178
caucus 83
cause and effect 98
Chancellorsville 167
checks and balances 56
   impeachment 57
   judicial appointments 57
   judicial review 57
   presidential nominees 57
   ratification of treaties 57
Chief Joseph 140
chief justice 64
Chinese Exclusion Act of 1882 42
citizenship 86
civil disobedience 83
Civil War 31, 163
   key battles 168, 169
   war time advantages 163
Clark, George Rogers 109
Clay, Henry 133, 149
committee 66
Committees of Correspondence 105
Common Sense 106
compromise 73, 84
Compromise of 1833 149
Compromise of 1850 159
Compromise of 1877 178
Confederate States of America 163
Congress
   power limit 59
Connecticut Plan 73
conservationists 34
Constitutional Convention 84, 98
constitutional monarchy 54
Continental Army 111
Cornwallis, General Lord 112
corrupt bargain 146
cotton gin 135
cotton kingdom 135
court
   supreme 64
   types of 64
   US court system 64
cowtowns 137
Crawford, William 146

Crazy Horse 139
Crockett, Davy 128
Cuba 88
Cumberland Road 134
Custer, George Armstrong 139

D
Davis, Jefferson 163
Dawes Act 141
Declaration of Independence 47, 75, 80, 106, 109
Deere, John 135
deforestation 34
Delaware River 110
delegate 61, 73, 114
Democrat 82
depression 147
diagram 23
diplomacy 87
direct democracy 53
Dix, Dorothea 152
doctrine of nullification 149
double jeopardy 76
Douglas, Stephen 162
Douglass, Frederick 153, 161
due process 76

E
economic interdependence 46
economic interest 90
economy
    agricultural 157
    industrial 158
education
    first public schools 151
    reform 151
egalitarianism 80
election
    1800 117
    1824 146
    1844 129
    1860 162
    general 83
    local 113
    recall 83
Electoral College 61, 114, 117
electoral map 21
Ellis Island 43
emancipation
    gradual 161
    immediate 160
Emancipation Proclamation 167
embargo 88
eminent domain 76
English Bill of Rights 79
Enlightenment 80
environment 46
Erie Canal 134
establishment clause 75
Europe
    Eastern 43
executive 56
executive branch 61, 62

F
faction 74
Federalist Papers 75
Federalists 74, 75
filibuster 66
First Battle of Bull Run 166
First Great Awakening 151

foreign policy 89
Fort McHenry 125
Fort Sumter 163
Fort Ticonderoga 109
Franklin Delano Roosevelt 61
Franklin, Benjamin 107
free exercise clause 75
Freedmen's Bureau 175
French and Indian War 29, 97
Fugitive Slave Law 159
Fulton, Robert 134

G
Gadsden Purchase 49, 131
Gadsden, James 49, 131
Garrison, William Lloyd 152
Gates, Horatio 110
geography 17, 28, 47, 49
Gettysburg Address 168
Ghost Dance 140
government
    absolute monarchy 54
    autocracy 54
    branches 73
    confederation 72
    constitutional monarchy 54
    dictatorship 54
    direct democracy 78
    federalism 55
    Greek influence 78
    limited 79
    oligarchy 54
    theocracy 54
    totalitarian 54
    types of 53
Grant, Ulysses S. 168, 171
graph, types of 23
Great Britain 29, 72, 80, 97, 103, 115, 126
Great Charter 79
Great Compromise 73
Great Migration 41
Great Plains 32, 135, 138
Green Mountain Boy 109
Greene, Nathanael 112
Grimke Sisters 152

H
Hamilton, Alexander 74, 114, 116
    duel with Burr 117
    economic plan 114
Hancock, John 108
Harper's Ferry 161
Hayes, Rutherford B 178
Henry, Patrick 108
historian 98, 100
historical data 101
Homestead Act 40, 132
House majority leader 59
House minority leader 59
House of Representatives 58
Houston, Sam 128
Howe, Julia Ward 154
humanitarian 87

I
immigrant 158
Immigrant
    German 42
    Jewish 43
    modern 45

impeachment 57, 62, 84
   President Johnson 174
impressment 116
inalienable rights 80
independents 82
Indian Removal 148
industrialization 40
infrastructure 134
   types of 134
interpretation (of Constitution)
   loose 74, 115
   strict 147
Intolerable Acts 105
Irish 42
isolationism 90

J

Jackson, Andrew 125, 128, 145
Jackson, Thomas "Stonewall" 167
Jacksonian Democracy 146
Jefferson, Thomas 31, 33, 48, 64, 75, 80, 107, 108, 114, 115, 117
   Republican party 116
John Deere's steel plow 135, 137
Johnson, Andrew 172
   impeachment 174
Joint Chiefs of Staff 63
judicial 56
judicial branch 64
judicial review 65

K

Kansas-Nebraska Act 160
King Andrew, 150
King George II 29
King George III 103, 149
Kitchen Cabinet 147
Ku Klux Klan 177

L

laissez-faire economics 147
law 59, 66
   constitutional process 66
Lee, Robert E 161, 166, 171
legislative branch 58
Lewis and Clark 33, 127
Lincoln, Abraham 130, 162, 167
Little Bighorn, Battle of 139
Locke, John 80
Louisiana Purchase 32, 48, 123
loyalists 104, 111

M

Madison, James 75, 124
Magna Carta 79
Manifest Destiny 49, 128, 130, 131, 148
Mann, Horace 151
map key 22
maps types of 17, 19, 20, 21
Marbury v. Madison 65
Marshall, John 65, 148
Mason-Dixon Line 31
Mayflower Compact 79
melting pot 43
mercantilism 46
Mexico 128
military 90
Mississippi River 31, 48, 125
Missouri Compromise 48, 159, 160
Monroe Doctrine 89, 126

Monroe, James 89, 126
Mormon 39
Morrill-Land Grant Act 132

N

national bank 115, 133
national convention 83
national debt 114
national security 90
Native American 29, 34, 97, 103, 127, 138
   assimilate 141
   Christianity 127
   relocation 139
   reservations 139
   violence against 139
nativists 158
natural rights 80
New Jersey Plan 73
New Orleans 31
   Battle of 32
Nez Perce 140
nomination of candidates 83
Northwest Ordinance 30
Northwest Territory 47, 123

O

Ohio River 29, 31, 47
Oregon Territory 33, 126, 129
Oregon Trail 33, 127

P

Paine, Thomas 106
Panic of 1819 134
parliament 79
patriots 104
Pierce, Franklin 49, 131
platform 82
political parties 149
   democrat 82
   Democratic-Republican 116
   Federalist 116, 125
   party platforms 82
   planks 82
   two-party system 150
   Whig 150
Polk, James 129
Polk, James K 49
popular sovereignty 159
population map 19
potato famine 158
power 62
   Congress 59
   delegated 55
precedence 64
Preemption Act 131
president of the United States 61
   cabinet 62
   qualifications 62
president pro tempore 59
presidential reconstruction 172
primary 83
prison reform 152
Proclamation of 1763 29
proclamation of neutrality 115
Promontory, Utah, 137
push and pull factors 43

Q

quartering 76

R

Radical Reconstruction 173
Radical Republican 173
railroad 136
    and farmers 137
    big business 136
    transcontinental 137
Reconstruction Act 177
Red Cloud 139
Red River Campaign 170
reform movement 151
rehabilitation 152
republic 53, 78
Republican Party 82, 162
Revolutionary War 150
right to bear arms 76
Rocky Mountains 32, 33, 40, 48
Roman influence 78

S

sanctions 88
Santa Anna, General Antonio 128
Saratoga 110
scalawag 178
Scott, Dred 160
Scott, General Winfield 130
secede 162
Second Battle of Bull Run 166
Second Continental Congress 72, 80
Second Great Awakening 151
secondary 100
secretary of defense 63
secretary of state 62, 89
sectionalism 133
Sedition Act 117
Senate 59
Senate majority leader 59
Senate minority leader 59
Seneca Falls Conference 153
Seventh Amendment 77
sharecropping 175
Shays, Daniel 72
Shays's Rebellion 72
Sherman, William T 169, 171
    march to the sea 169
Sitting Bull 140
slave trade compromise 73
slavery 30, 40, 47, 48, 73, 98, 159
    abolition 161
    recruited slaves 111
    slave society 157
Slidell, John 130
social contract theory 80
Sons of Liberty 104
South Carolina Nullification Crisis 149
Southern War 111
Spain 127
speaker of the House 58
spoils system 146
Stamp Act 104
Stanton, Edwin 174
Stanton, Elizabeth Cady 153
Star Spangled Banner 125, 158
state constitution 113
states' rights 98, 149
Statue of Liberty 43
steamboat 134, 136
Stevens, Thaddeus 174
strict interpretation (Constitution) 74, 115
suffrage 146

summit 89
Sumner, Charles 160
Supreme Court 64

T

tariff 88, 114, 133
    protective 133
Tea Act 105
temperance movement 153
tenant farmers 175
tenement 44
Tenure in Office Act 174
territorial map 17
Texas 128
The Alamo 128
theocracy 54
third party 82
Thomas, Jesse B. 48
Three-Fifths Compromise 73
Ticonderoga 111
timeline 95
topographical map 20
Townshend Acts 105
trade (free) 88
Trail of Tears 148
Transcontinental Railroad 34
treaty 87
Treaty of Ghen 125
Treaty of Guadalupe-Hidalgo 49, 130
Treaty of Paris 112
Truth, Sojourner 154
Tubman, Harriet 161
two-party system 82
Tyler, John 129

U

Underground Railroad 31, 161
United Nations 91
United States Constitution 54, 59, 61, 62, 65, 74, 78, 98, 115
urbanization 40
    modern 45
    negative consequences 44

V

Valley Forge 111
veto 56
    override 56
vice president 61
    responsibilities 62
Vicksburg 168
Virginia Plan 73
voting 83

W

Walker, David 153
War for Independence 111
War of 1812 125, 135
War with Mexico 130
Washington, George 106, 110, 114
    farewell address 116
Webster, Daniel 149
Whiskey Rebellion 115
White League 177
Women's Rights Movement. 153
Wounded Knee 140

Y

Yellowstone National Park 34